Questions you're NOT supposed to ask

Tony Williams

NH
NEW HOLLAND

First published in 2009 by New Holland Publishers (NZ) Ltd
Auckland • Sydney • London • Cape Town

www.newhollandpublishers.co.nz

218 Lake Road, Northcote, Auckland 0627, New Zealand
Unit 1, 66 Gibbes Street, Chatswood, NSW 2067, Australia
86–88 Edgware Road, London W2 2EA, United Kingdom
80 McKenzie Street, Cape Town 8001, South Africa

Packaged for New Holland Publishers by Oratia Media, Auckland
(www.oratiamedia.com)

Design: Cheryl Rowe
Editorial: Carolyn Lagahetau, Sam Hill and Frances Chan

National Library of New Zealand Cataloguing-in-Publication Data
Williams, Tony, 1960-
Questions you're not supposed to ask / Tony Williams.
ISBN 978-1-86966-276-9
1. Life—Miscellanea. 2. Life—Humor. I. Title.
128—dc 22

1 3 5 7 9 10 8 6 4 2

Printed in China at Everbest Printing Co., on paper sourced from sustainable forests.

Contents

Acknowledgements

Thanks to my mother for her hospitality and feeding me full to the brim. And to Lynda Scott who also provided hospitality during the writing of it.

Thank you to Peter Dowling of Oratia Media for setting up the book and being a valued friend, to New Holland for commissioning it, to editor Carolyn Lagahetau for her wise patience and to Richard Gunther for his irreverent cartoons. Thanks to any others who have contributed, many of whom were involved in the production process and are unknown to me.

Thanks also to that most undervalued yet reliable of all professionals — the librarian.

But most of all, THANKS TO YOU for dipping into your pocket and coming out with your hard-earned cash to buy this book. I hope you have good fun reading it and that it will help you in this woolly adventure we call life.

Chapter 0
The Power of Knowledge

Why does this book begin at Chapter 0?

 Because everything actually begins from nothing.

First question, please.

Q: What is sex?
A: Hold on a moment, hadn't we better explain what this book is all about first?

This book answers the questions you are not supposed to ask about sex, money, governments, taxation and so on, and it also answers the questions you maybe should have asked, tried to ask or in fact DID ask, but never got a proper answer to. The intention is to arm you with knowledge.

❓ Q: Why isn't knowledge freely available?
■ A: It should be, but throughout history knowledge has been suppressed.

> *You cannot teach a man anything.*
> *You can only help him discover it within himself.*
> — Galileo

As you know, the Earth is flat. Yes it is, don't argue with me. And the Sun revolves around the Earth. Yes, it does. This is the Middle Ages and the Roman Catholic Church has a monopoly on all knowledge.

That's right, knowledge is not free to share, but is owned by an Authority and of course they are right because they say they are right.

With logical calculation and thought, however, Polish astronomer Nicolaus Copernicus dared to contend that the Earth actually revolved around the Sun.

When the great scientist Galileo Galilei, after proper observation and calculation, supported Copernicus' theory, he was tortured by agents of the Inquisition and forced to recant. He spent his last days under house arrest, eventually going blind.

❓ Q: Why did they treat him like that?
■ A: Because he asked a question he was not supposed to ask.

❓ Q: Surely, this is an isolated example?
■ A: Hardly! The anatomist Andreas Vesalius was accused of murdering a dead person.

When Vesalius started dissecting corpses in the sixteenth century, the authority on the human body was still considered to be Claudius Galen, a Roman physician and philosopher who had been born in Greece.

Galen had said the breastbone was composed of seven parts; however, Vesalius could find only three. Galen had also said the liver had lobes, but Vesalius could not find any.

Finally, it dawned on Vesalius that Galen had never even dissected a human body (at the time Galen had only been allowed to dissect monkeys). So to discover the truth, Vesalius embarked on more dissections. It was hard to find willing corpses (and even harder to find relatives of the deceased who would willingly grant permission) so he often dissected the bodies of convicts who had been hanged.

Vesalius published his findings in a book containing over 300 detailed drawings. This led to an uproar when his findings contradicted those of Galen. Vesalius had asked questions he was not supposed to ask. Worse still, he had gone against an Established Authority. He was accused of murder since during one dissection he had discovered the heart was still beating.

So vehement was the wave of opposition that Vesalius threw a large part of his manuscript into the fire. Yet today he is recognised as the father of modern anatomy.

Q: Why would anyone want to suppress knowledge?
A: For money.

In Europe during the Middle Ages, kings, aristocrats and priests conspired to keep the general populace illiterate and, therefore, poor.

Every month the priests preached a sermon to the masses that the monarch ruled by divine right. It was a case of '... and now a word from our sponsors' since it was the people (peasants) who actually did the work.

The kings, the aristocracy and the priests took their cut for creating (what was partly) an illusion that they actually did something important.

This continued until 1440 when German goldsmith Johannes Gutenberg invented the printing press.

As books became more widely available, a reading revolution was sparked, arming people with the knowledge to democratically claim their rights.

Q: So we solved the problem, didn't we?
A: Um ... did you ever read George Orwell's masterpiece *Animal Farm*?

In the story, the animals, who have hitherto been the workers, take over the farmyard so that 'all animals are equal'; but the pigs eventually become the new ruling class because, they claim, 'some animals are more equal than others'.

Unfortunately the history of knowledge is that some group will declare themselves a New Authority to try to control people and therefore money, so beware those who claim to have the monopoly on knowledge.

Q: Who is the New Authority?
A: Governmental bodies, educational institutions and the mass media.

All of these organisations try to tell us how to think: the mass media is controlled by the financial power of advertisers ('And now a word from our sponsor'); education is funded by government ('And now a word from our sponsor'); and governments attempt to tell us how to think and act ('And now a law from our sponsor').

Q: Isn't that a harsh way of looking at it?
A: The truth is sometimes a little brutal.

It is far better to be brutal with words than to let people suffer the brutality that life can visit upon them when they are kept in ignorance. The first duty of a writer is to write the truth; only that way can you right wrongs.

But neither should knowledge be dull and serious. The pursuit of knowledge is meant to be fun and this book is written with irreverence and attitude.

Q: Where is the true information available?
A: From people themselves and from books.

People are perceptive. Whenever I have talked to those who were witness to a reported event, they have given me far more useful first-hand information than the news articles did. Books written by independent minds provide knowledge that enlightens and empowers.

Q: So is there any 'authority' we can look to for guidance?
A: Intuitive knowledge.

There is a kind of intuitive knowledge that runs through language, seen when words are traced back to their original meanings. Such as the word 'mystery', derived from the Greek *myein* meaning 'to close' and *mystes*, a title given to initiates of ancient secret societies.

Mystery originally referred to keeping secrets, closing the eyes and lips of the initiates and preventing them from revealing details about their religious ceremonies, thereby concealing knowledge of the rites from those who were not members.

So the knowledge was kept within a select group, hidden away, not broadly available. Knowledge can be used either to control people or to set them free.

This book aims to set you free.

Q: Are all the subjects here taboo?
A: No.

The book also fills in missing data, interprets confusing data and corrects false data. It asks the questions to give a clearer picture of who you are and how life fits in with you (not how you fit in with life).

Q: How does the book work?
A: It starts with subjects you are most familiar with — such as money and sex — and ends up at the other end of the universe with the Big Questions such as, Who is God?

Q: So who decides what is right?
A: There is only one person who can truly decide that.

It is you.

Chapter 1
The Human Being

This first section is dedicated to you, the individual.

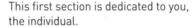

Sex

Finally, some sex!

What is sex?

A **Be patient. We have to introduce the subject properly first.**

Historically, sex is probably the most taboo subject that exists. We are mostly supposed to learn about it by trial and error, schoolyard gossip and what we deduce at the movies. There is also a risk that young people will resort to pornographic sources to gain information. What follows is a quick summary of the 'Facts of Life' or 'The Birds and the Bees', which you may or may not have had access to when you were a teenager. Maybe you have worked it all out by now; at the very least you might have a few laughs as you have some fond memories of learning about this pleasant absurdity known as sex.

? Q: What is sex?
■ A: A method of furthering a species.

Humans do it. Animals do it too. Trees and plants don't (not in the same way anyway — have you ever seen two trees hugging?). There was once a primitive tribe that decided that sex was bad and banned it. For some reason that tribe no longer exists.

Humans also do it for pleasure. Along with dolphins, the human race is the only species that actually has sex for pleasure.

◇ A pair of Indian pythons was once observed copulating for 180 days.

◇ Eagles can have sex while flying at 60 miles (96 km) an hour. It is not uncommon for both birds to hit the ground before they finish. Now that's a landing!

◇ The desert rat mates 222 times an hour. *Whoa!*

◇ Some lions mate more than 50 times a day.

All these animals are doing it to increase their species.

? Q: Why is sex so pleasurable?
■ A: It's cunningly designed by nature to be enjoyed.

The truth is that some people are not so attractive. In fact, some are plug ugly. Plus there are people who do not want to put up with having a nagging partner or raise a noisy brood of children. These things cost money and take up time that could be spent engaged in more valuable activities such as fishing, sunbathing or sticking stamps in stamp albums. But sex has been designed so that the urge is so strong and the pleasure to be derived so great that most people end up doing it anyway.

❓ Q: What makes it so pleasurable?
A: It's really a form of tickling.

The body communicates with its parts through the nerves, which transmit vibrations through the body using electrical impulses. When something comes into contact with these nerve endings, a feeling is transmitted through them. If the contact is too strong or intense, pain shoots up the nerve channels. If the contact is gentle, pleasure transmits. Sexual contact tends to involve a lighter, more delicate pressure — rather like getting tickled — and the best places to tickle are the erogenous zones.

❓ Q: What are the erogenous zones?
A: The love zones.

In both men and women the erogenous zones are usually the genital areas. The word genital comes from *gignere*, which means 'to create offspring'. Erogenous comes from the Greek goddess *Eros* who was the patron of love, and *-genous* meaning 'causing'; therefore erogenous literally means 'making love'. Essentially, the erogenous zones are the penis (for men) and the vagina (for women). A woman's breasts are also considered erogenous zones as they provide sexual pleasure when touched.

A multitude of tiny nerve endings are clustered closely together in the erogenous zones and like the fine strings of a piano, when played gently, they make sweet music.

❓ Q: Apart from all the fun is there an underlying purpose to sex?
A: It promotes diversity.

Actually, the world would be a lot more boring without sex. No seriously, I mean it. *The world would be a lot more boring without sex.* There would be no blondes or brunettes or redheads. There would just be billions of people who looked exactly the same. A single cell reproduces by splitting and making an exact duplicate of itself. Boring!

The joy of sex is that with two parties involved there is an infinite set of possibilities so we end up with the variety that is the spice of life. That's probably why some people consider sex to be the spice of life.

Q: So how do you actually get sex?
A: First, you have to make contact with someone you are attracted to.

There is a basic law of this universe that opposites attract. Not only that, but it also creates the potential for energy to flow between the two opposite terminals. That's how electricity is created, flowing between positive and negative terminals, or how a storm is generated between ridges of high and low pressure.

That's also how romantic relationships are created and why they sometimes flash like lightning and are as dramatic and passionate as a storm.

Q: What makes a person attractive?
A: Beauty is designed to attract.

Flowers are pretty for a reason: to attract the bees that will transfer their pollen. Beauty sends out subtle little 'come hither' messages. It makes the world seem more pleasant and you want to get closer to it. In the natural world, beauty leads to reproduction.

In human terms, beauty is entirely a matter of opinion. Years ago the ideal woman was supposed to be pear-shaped. Now she is supposed to look like a stick insect. However, there is an old proverb that says, 'Beauty is in the eye of the beholder' and another that says, 'Beauty comes from within'.

The great beauty and actress Sophia Loren once said that you have to 'think yourself beautiful'.

Q: So what's the first step?
A: Usually eye contact.

You see them. Maybe they see you. Maybe there is a glint of interest in their eye. A lot of people believe in love at first sight; however this is

often a delusion, since there is a lot more to a person than simply their appearance — they might have some very annoying habits that you just don't know about yet. Certainly, there either is an immediate attraction or there isn't.

It should be obvious to you how you feel about them, but usually it is less obvious to you how they feel about you, and that is part of the fun.

❓ Q: What's the next step?
■ A: Communication has to take place.

There are a lot of very clever chat-up lines that are reputed to work, though it is usually better simply to chat in a normal friendly, introductory way, with a little bit of humour, and if possible, wit. This usually leads to sharing some viewpoints, exchanging contact details and an agreement about the next time you will meet. This could simply be a friendship to start with or — if there is open romantic intent — a 'first date'.

15

❓ Q: Can't we just speed this up right now and get to the sex?

■ **A: Okay, if you insist. We'll have sex first and a relationship later.**

❓ Q: What's the first point of sexual contact?

■ **A: The kiss!**

Be warned: kissing burns 26 calories a minute!

In many cultures, a kiss on the cheek is an acceptable form of greeting. In most cultures a kiss directly on the lips is considered to be sexual.

As the kiss becomes more passionate, the mouth may be opened and each partner may probe their tongue into the mouth of the other. This is known as French kissing (probably because for years the demure English only kissed on the outside of the lips, if at all). In American culture, it is known as getting to first base, as in baseball.

For those not familiar with the game, the batter hits a ball and tries to run around four bases. If the ball is struck right out of the park, that is a home run and the batter can jog around the bases accepting the applause of the crowd. With sex, the intention is also to hit a home run.

❓ Q: What follows the kiss?

■ **A: Foreplay.**

Foreplay is when one party touches the other's body in a sexual way. This usually commences with a non-erogenous zone, such as stroking an arm. This then proceeds to the erogenous zones. Caressing of the female breasts is known as 'getting to second base'. Some other popular names for breasts are boobs, melons, bazookas, tits, knockers, whoppers, sizzlers, balloons, pillows, drums and hooters; the list is almost endless!

❓ Q. Now we are getting somewhere. What's next?

■ **A. Foreplay with the genital areas.**

Foreplay can involve the full or partial removal of the other person's clothes.

If both parties are in a hurry to hit a home run, this can be done with abandon. But it can also be very stimulating if this stage is done in a slow, teasing and suspenseful way.

The stimulation of the genital areas can either be done as a separate activity in itself, or as preparation for lovemaking.

Q: What is the genital region of a man?
A: The penis and testicles.

The penis is also known by many other names including the cock, dick, willy, love pump, rod of love, knob, pecker, the one-eyed snake and the general.

The testicles, also known as the balls, nuts, bollocks, stones, cojones and crown jewels, manufacture semen. They are not particularly sensitive to touch.

The penis is very sensitive to touch. When aroused, blood flows into it, causing it to stiffen and become erect. Other names for an erection include boner, woody, stiffie and hard-on.

Q: What is the genital region of a woman?
A: The vagina.

Like a man's penis, during sexual arousal a woman's vagina will expand in both length and width.

The vagina is also known as the vajayjay, pussy, pudji, muffin, toolbox, juice box, tunnel of love, muff and poonani.

Q: What is a clitoris?
A: A little bud of joy.

A clitoris is a small, erectile bud located near the entrance to the woman's vagina. It is highly sensitive and is a source of great pleasure to a woman.

The walls of the vagina are also very sensitive to touch.

Q: How do you stimulate the woman's genital area?
A: Gently and lovingly.

You can caress the vagina externally and then insert a finger and caress internally. At this point, the vagina releases natural lubrication, moistening it. The woman will reach a point where her breasts are swollen, her nipples are erect, the clitoris is erect and the lips of the vagina are relaxed and have opened.

This is called 'getting to third base' and the woman is physically prepared for intercourse.

For his part, a man should feel a sense of excitement and anticipation and his penis should be erect.

Intercourse can now take place.

Q: What is a hymen?
A: A ring of thin issue at the entrance to the vagina when a woman is a virgin. If a woman is sufficiently aroused, this will normally break by the insertion of the penis into her vagina.

Q: What is fellatio?
A: Sexual stimulation of the penis using the mouth and lips.

Fellatio comes from the Latin *fellare* meaning 'to suck'. Another common term for it is a blow job.

Q: What is cunnilingus?
A: Sexual stimulation of the vagina using the mouth and lips.

Cunnilingus comes from the Latin *cunnus* meaning 'vulva' and *lingere* meaning 'to lick'.

Fellatio and cunnilingus are also referred to as oral sex.

Q: Wait, what about protection?
A: Yes, protect yourself and others.

Condoms are used to stop the spread of sexually transmitted infections (STI). They are also used as a contraceptive measure.

People who are in monogamous relationships (they only have sex with each other) therefore do not need to use condoms if they use a different form of contraception, or none at all if they want to conceive children.

Condoms have been around for thousands of years; some of the earliest condoms were made from the lining of a sheep's stomach.

❓ Q: Can we start now?
A: Yes. Proceed straight to 'fourth base.'

This is also known as making love (usually the preferred term by females), f***ing, shagging, bonking, nookie, getting nailed, getting laid, having it off, having it away and a bit of how's your father?

❓ Q: What is orgasm?
A: The home run.

The sensation of orgasm is a feeling of complete physical ecstasy. The word orgasm comes from the Greek *organ* meaning 'to swell'. Climax, another term for orgasm, comes from the Greek word for a ladder, so in other words, achieving climax is to 'reach the top of the ladder'.

For men, orgasm involves the ejaculation of the semen out of the penis. Ejaculation comes from the Latin '*ex*', (out) and '*jacere*' (throw), literally to 'throw out'. This is the main point of orgasm for a man and ends the lovemaking for him.

❓ Q: Is it the same for a woman?
A: No. Reportedly it's even more intense.

A woman does not always achieve orgasm during intercourse, but when she does, she usually experiences a feeling of suspense, then intense pleasure concentrated at first on the clitoris, then spreading through the pelvic area accompanied by rhythmic contractions of the outer two-thirds of her vagina. The more contractions there are, the more intense is the orgasm. This sensation can last from a few seconds to several minutes. Then a strong sensation of pleasure, described as a feeling of warmth, spreads throughout her whole body resulting in a sense of peace and relaxation.

? Q: What's the best way to ensure that a woman achieves orgasm?
A: By being patient.

Since the penis usually goes flaccid after orgasm, where possible, it is good manners for a man to hold off his own orgasm until the woman has achieved hers. Each partner can then reach orgasm simultaneously, which is very satisfying. Some women can achieve multiple orgasms.

Orgasm can also be achieved by stimulation of the vagina by fingers or by cunnilingus, and some women have been known to achieve orgasm without any sexual contact at all.

? Q: How can a man tell when a woman achieves orgasm?
A: There are a couple of options.

A. By observation of the above indicators.

B. By asking her.

However, if a man is making love in Connersville, Wisconsin, and he suspects his female partner has achieved orgasm, he should not fire a gun in celebration as it is against the law there to do so. In this case, the meaning of the word 'gun' is quite literal.

? Q: Is that it then? Is it all over?
A: No, there's still the aftermath.

You still have to jog around the bases, accepting the applause of the crowd, which means to say some partners don't like it when their lover goes straight to sleep after sex. Sometimes a few words or a form of affection is needed to show the other that they are valued for who they are, not just the pleasure their body imparts.

Alternatively return to 'Go' and start again!

Money

> *Annual income £20, annual expenditure £19/6, result happiness.*
> *Annual income £20, annual expenditure £20/6, result misery.*
> — *Mr Micawber in* David Copperfield *by Charles Dickens*

No two subjects obsess adult thinking more than sex and money. Sex is the contact point of romantic relationships, and money is the contact point between the individual and society. And where there is contact, there is friction.

There is one question about money that people want to know more than any other:

How do I get to be rich?

 By working hard and knowing the laws of money.

In the musical *Fiddler on the Roof*, the impoverished Topol sings an agonising prayer to his god that if he were a rich man, he wouldn't have to work hard. In truth, to get to be rich, you have to work hard. Work hard, but work smart.

Q: So what is money?
A: Money is a form of invisible energy.

As such, it follows the laws of energy. Think of money as water:

> when it rains, that is income;

> when it pools in a reservoir, that is your piggy bank.

But you are certain there are holes in your system because the level always seems to be going down. There are leaks and your money will find them because, like all other forms of energy, money follows the path of least resistance.

? Q: Why is how much money you have so important?

A: Because money measures production.

Production is making something that others consider valuable. Originally, people only made enough for their own use but then they started making more than they needed and exchanging it with each other. This was the birth of barter.

A farmer bred pigs. His wife baked cakes, which he liked. She was out of flour so he went and swapped one of his pigs for a bag of flour. The problem was deciding how many bags he got for one pig. Also, he had to drag the pig around with him in order to exchange it. Obviously what was needed was some portable medium of exchange — a token.

Money is simply a token that keeps the score, as in a sports contest. Except it keeps the score of your life.

? Q: So then they started printing paper money?

A: Hold on a minute — they had not even invented paper yet.

In parts of Africa, shells were used as tokens, while Native American Indians used wampum (threaded beads or discs made from shells). In Gujarat, India they used almond seeds, and in Haiti, tree gourds.

Other forms of money included animal hides, salt, cloth, pots, jewels, animal teeth, horns, skins, jawbones of pigs, and slaves.

In the Iron Age, metal became the preferred token. Metals were durable and were rare. In Sparta, they used iron rods as money. The people of Lydia, a kingdom in western Asia Minor, were the first to melt metal down into coins in about 650 BC, stamping them with the portrait of the king.

At first, coins were worth their actual weight, but then those crafty kings realised they could double their money by melting a cheaper metal into the mix and so money became devalued, and that was when it started becoming not a commodity but an idea.

Q: Where did the word 'money' come from?
A: It was coined by a gaggle of geese.

Some invaders tried to sneak into Rome late one night and upset these geese, which became so annoyed and made such a commotion that they roused a sleeping Roman, Manlius Capolinus. He raised the alarm and Rome was saved.

The Romans were so grateful that they knocked down Capolinus' house (some thanks!) and built a temple on it in honour of the goddess Juno the Monitress who monitored (watched over) Rome.

Later, the temple was converted into a mint where the most valuable coins were made, and so the name Monitress got altered to *moneta* and this became the word 'money'.

Q: Who invented paper money?
A: Those clever Chinese. But first they had to invent paper.

By about 812 AD the Chinese people got fed up with lugging bags of coins around with them when they went shopping. Instead, they started leaving the coins with shopkeepers, who would give them a receipt.

People began to swap these receipts among themselves, so paper became a token for the money and soon afterwards, Chinese authorities started printing paper money.

One note from the reign of the Emperor Hung-Wu (1368–98 AD) which survives bears the warning 'counterfeiters will be beheaded'.

Q: How was plastic money invented?
A: Plastic money or charge cards were invented in the US in the 1920s.

Paper is as light as a feather, but it still takes up room in the wallet. In the US during the 1920s hotels and oil companies started using plastic cards to record purchases and this was the birth of credit cards.

These days we have electronic transactions, so that in many cases it would seem as though the token has disappeared again, but that's hardly a problem since money has only ever been an idea anyway — what counts is the production behind it.

Q: Why are credit cards so easy to obtain?
A: Because they charge a much higher rate of interest than a normal bank loan.

They charge so much interest that they would even give a card to a dog. This happened in the US after an owner filled in an application form using their dog's name. The fantastic plastic came back with the name of the pet imprinted on it. Occupation: *dog*. His credit limit was probably 1000 bones.

Q: What is the purpose of money?
A: To get things done.

Money is one of the few things that everybody agrees on. If you wanted somebody to clean the (expletive deleted) out of your drains, nobody would want to do it unless you paid them. We get money by doing something we often don't want to do, to get money to do something we do want to do. Money is not an end in itself. It is only a vehicle to get things done.

Q: What does money give the user?
A: Freedom of choice.

? Q: What is the golden rule of money?

A: The person with the gold makes the rules.

? Q: Why do I never seem to have enough money?

A: Because you can never have *enough*.

As soon as you do, you spend it and then you don't have enough again. In Romany, the language of the gypsies, there is no word for *enough*. They simply do not have the idea that anything is ever enough. You can never have enough money. So in truth people either have *not enough* or *too much*. Not having enough is often considered to be poverty.

? Q: So what's being rich?

A: Having *more* than enough.

Enough is never really enough. To survive you actually need too much. That is what rich and wealthy mean.

The word 'rich' comes from Old English *rice* meaning 'having more than enough'. The word 'wealth' comes from Old English *well* or *weal*, meaning 'well-being'. These states give you financial security.

Security comes from the Latin *se* or 'from' and *cura* or 'care; without having to worry'. The word 'luxury' comes from the Latin *luxus* meaning 'abundance'. Abundance comes from the Latin *abundare* or 'to overflow'. So the only guarantee in life is a dancing bun ... I mean a bun dance ... I mean abundance.

? Q: How do I control money?

A: You have to or it will control you.

Either money is running your life or you are using money to have the life you want. How much money you have is immaterial. What really matters is that you are in control of it.

The Spanish have a saying, 'No es más feliz aquel que más tiene; si no aquel que menos necesita', which roughly translates as 'The happiest person is not the one who has the most, but who needs the least.'

❓ Q: Come on, stop beating around the bush. How do I get rich?
A: By using money to extend your survival potential longer into the future.

Originally, the human race survived solely by hunting and gathering. Often they would only get enough food to last a day. Then they found ways of preserving their food a little longer by cooking it (preserving was the original purpose of cooking) or by salting it, pickling it and other methods. From there humans learned how to grow crops, which effectively extended their survival potential to a year.

So the first step to wealth is to get off the daily grind and start planning ahead. Stop being a consumer and spending your money on consumables that last less than a day — junk food, drink, cigarettes and so on — and start investing in things that will take the money further into the future.

❓ Q: What is investment?
A: Investment is using money to make money.

Investment is putting something in now, to get something back in the future. The word 'investment' comes from the Latin *vestire* meaning 'to clothe', or in other words, putting your shirt on it.

There are investments other than money. One is time. Another is good manners. If used wisely, money, time and manners will bring good returns. Time creates leisure time, manners create goodwill and money begets money.

Q: What is the first law of investment?
A: Always protect your capital.

Capital is the money you have available to use to make more money. It comes from the Latin *caput* for 'head', because the original measure of wealth was counting the heads of your flock.

Q: What are the key principles of investment?
A: First, understand what you are investing in.

This is the key principle of Warren Buffet, the world's greatest investor, and he didn't do badly to have a net worth in the billions. Don't deceive yourself by believing that things will come right because of luck or optimism or some airy-fairy idea you have. Fully investigate what you are investing in until you understand it and have isolated a very real and tangible reason why the investment will increase in value.

Q: Any other investment tips?
A: Here are a few quick pearls.

◇ A small safe return is better than a risk.

◇ Invest in things that have potential for growth.

◇ Never be in a hurry to invest.

◇ Spread the risk.

◇ Refuse far more investments than you take.

Q: How successful will I be as an investor?
A: That depends on you. One investor said that on average, out of every ten investments made, one or two are wonderful, four or five are moderately successful and the rest will be disasters.

? Q: How do you store wealth?
■ A: By solidifying liquid cash flow into solid assets.

Just as you can store water by freezing it into ice, in financial terms, you can store money as assets.

Money can flow out just as fast as it can flow in, because in its cash form it is in a liquid state. To protect and hang on to it, you have to solidify cash into assets.

Asset comes from the Latin *ad* meaning 'to', and *satis* or 'enough'. In other words, you have enough money to allow it to sit down and take a rest for a while.

? Q: What is the basic principle behind assets?
■ A: The more solid the asset, the longer it will endure.

The Earth endures, so buy a patch of it. Mark Twain said, 'Invest in land, because they ain't making any more of it.' Gold and diamonds are both considered very valuable. Apart from the beauty of their physical appearance, diamonds are very hard, whereas gold is dense and heavy.

Though stocks and shares are pieces of paper, they represent holdings in companies that usually own considerable and very enduring assets. The biggest asset in any company is its management (if they are good).

The key to all this is ownership and therefore, though not physical, enduring ownership rights have great value. A few years ago, Disney Studios renewed the licence for Winnie the Pooh from the estate of A.A. Milne for tens of millions of dollars. The popularity of the little bear endures.

Art is also something that holds its value, especially after the artist has died, since each artwork is unique and therefore rare, and this scarcity naturally increases once the artist dies.

Q: How do you know what to charge for something?
A: You charge what the market will bear.

This means charge as much as you can until just before the point that people would stop buying. Although any young child — children usually have a very high sense of justice — would probably tell you that this is unfair, it is in fact the only way for a business to guarantee its survival.

Q: What controls the amount of money I make?
A: Demand.

A Canadian civil servant once visited an Inuit community in the far north. Because they did not trade much in money, however, the man realised they were eligible for welfare payments. At first the Inuit were very happy to accept the government's free cash, but then the Inuit elders noticed that canning and fur outputs were dropping and people were getting sick and lazy. They stopped the welfare cheques and production and morale returned to their former levels.

Demand determines income.

Q: Will anything else help me make more money?
A: Communication.

Communication is incredibly important. It goes by many names including promotion, advertising, public relations, sales, circulating and networking. They all add up to getting out a flow of communication that interests people in what you are doing.

Q: What does communication produce?
A: Relationships.

Other people are very valuable to your wealth and through communication you form relationships with them. Never underestimate how much knowledge or power even the apparently humble cleaner or receptionist might hold, or how helpful they can be. A friendly greeting, treating everyone with good manners and showing respect can produce incalculable results.

? Q: What do relationships produce?

■ **A: Opportunities.**

The word 'opportunity' comes from the Latin *op* or 'towards' and *portus* meaning 'harbour', in other words, the wind is favourably driving the ship towards the harbour. Therefore you have to take opportunities immediately they present themselves — before the wind changes again.

? Q: When I've got money, how do I hang on to it?

■ **A: By budgeting.**

Some people think budgeting is a swear word, but it just means financial planning. It comes from the Latin *bursa* which means 'a purse'; when the purse is empty, you are in trouble. It's budget or bodge it. Some people think of budgeting as boring, but how about this for creative budgeting? In English cricket, one of the greatest challenges is for a player to score 1000 runs as a batsman and 100 wickets in a season. In 1984, when the great New Zealand all-rounder Richard Hadlee set this as a goal, it had not been achieved for nearly two decades (partly due to the playing season being shortened). But Hadlee did something very clever. Before the season began, he budgeted it out.

Budget	Result
He budgeted to play in at least 20 matches.	He played in 24.
He budgeted 31 innings.	He played 33.
He budgeted 750 overs.	He bowled 772.
He needed 1000 runs.	He scored 1179.
He needed 100 wickets.	He took 117.

So he did it.

? Q: What's the most important rule in budgeting?

■ **A: Consider all the bills together before you pay any one of them.**

Q: What is the most important phrase in the English language?
A: No, it's not 'I love you'. It's 'under budget'.

Q: Will I get wealthy by going into business?
A: You can, but ...

Running a business requires a survival instinct that gets trained out of most people at school, which is probably why a lot of successful people in business did not stay long at school.

Running a business is a bit like being the captain of a ship. There are so many aspects of it you have to know and so it is usually better to start small, borrow little and grow it in response to your success and failures on a daily basis.

In fact, many businesses achieve success almost accidentally, after finding a need and fulfilling it. Roughly 50% of the success of any business is in finding that need. It sounds simple, but getting that right (and selling it right) is the difference between success and disaster.

You have to be prepared to work long hours (sometimes very long hours) and to be a leader. You have to continually keep learning and stay alert, because it is what you don't know or don't see that will bite you. Having said all that, there are few better feelings than being your own boss and master of your own destiny.

Q: But how do I become filthy, stinking rich?
A: By parlaying and geometric progression.

Q: What is parlaying?
A: Making use of an asset or advantage to make a further success.

Parlay comes from the Latin *parare* which means 'prepare'. In parlaying, you use your existing stake to turn it into a bigger stake. For example, a salesperson's trick after a sale is to ask the purchaser for the names of three friends who would also be interested in the product.

❓ Q: What is geometric progression?
A: Geometric progression is the principle of growing something in relation to its existing size.

The difference between parlaying and geometric progression is that parlaying tends to be taking the opportunity of the moment, while geometric progression is more of a planned strategy of growth over a period of time.

A good example of geometric progression is the story of the Chinese peasant who performed a beneficial act for the emperor. When the emperor asked what he wanted in return, the peasant replied a single grain of rice, doubled every day for 30 days. By the end of the month the peasant had a barn full of rice and was a very rich man.

Sam Walton was just a single individual who started the Wal-Mart chain of stores. Today, it has two million employees. Here is the scale of its growth by geometric progression.

Year	Stores	Turnover (US$)
1946	1	105,000
1960	9	1.4 m
1970	32	31 m
1972	51	78 m
1974	78	168 m
1976	125	340 m
1978	195	678 m
1980	276	1.2 bn
1990	1528	26 bn
2008	7000	340 bn

So Sam did all right, didn't he?

Success

Genius is 1% inspiration and 99% perspiration.
— *Thomas Edison*

We all want to be successful in our lives. Everyone will have their own judgement of what success is. The word itself comes from the Latin *suc* meaning 'to' and *cedere* 'or go'; therefore to go towards or achieve.

How can I guarantee that I will be successful?

A **The best way is to repeat the common factors of successful people.**

A factor is something that produces a result. Once you know the factors of something you can produce the same result. Factor comes from the Latin *facere*, 'to make or do'.

Q: So what's the most obvious factor of successful people?
A: Hard work.

Sometimes they work very hard for a long period of time, struggling or failing. Sometimes the hard work seems to go on and on. Colonel Sanders of Kentucky Fried Chicken fame was a pensioner before he started his business.

There is a formula that it takes a lot of hard work to get a little bit of success, then a little bit of hard work to get a lot of success. People are sometimes heralded by the media as an overnight success. But in reality there is no such thing. Even teenage singing stars have put in hours and hours of practice as a child.

If the term *hard work* sounds too much like hard work, however, you can also call it *creativity*.

? Q: What's the next most noticeable factor?
A: Method.

Hard work was such an obvious factor in people's success that it took me an infuriatingly long time to work out the next one, which was actually staring me in the face all the time. There seemed to be a bewildering array of ways that people were successful. While one acquired wealth by borrowing to the hilt, another would not borrow at all. I could find no common method.

Finally, it dawned on me: the common denominator was that they each had a method. Their own method. Usually they had worked it out by trial and error — sometimes it was even a little quirky — but the most important factor was that it worked.

So you have to find a method that works for you.

? Q: What's the most important factor?
A: Strength of purpose.

Just because I discovered hard work and method first does not mean they are the most important. The most important factor is strength of purpose.

Purpose is knowing the intended result and having the intention to achieve it. The word comes from the Latin *pro* meaning 'forward', and pose or put; to place forward. 'Intend' comes from the Latin *in* meaning 'towards' and *tendere*, 'to stretch or reach; to reach towards'. Intention is the archer taking aim at the bull's eye.

Purpose is an ongoing thing. It is taking aim every day.

? Q: How do you maintain purpose?
A: Focus.

Success has a very narrow focus.

The word 'focus' comes directly from Latin and refers to a fireplace or a hearth, meaning that all the light and heat is generating from one point. An individual is the same when fully focused, harnessing all their power, ability and clarity of perception towards one point or goal.

Life has many distractions — some good, some bad — and it is essential to maintain focus. I had a friend who served in the Second World War as a fighter pilot and never felt fear because he had tremendous focus. As he explained, 'I found that what I used to do was just focus completely on the task without any distractions. I used to just block everything out of my mind except the task at hand, and then at the end of the day when the missions were completed, I would go back and relax.'

Q: How do you overcome failures and setbacks?
A: Persistence.

> *Life consists of moving from defeat to defeat*
> *to defeat without loss of enthusiasm.*
> — *Winston Churchill*

Persistence is the antidote to failure. The word comes from the Latin *per* or 'through' and *sistere*, 'to make stand; to be strong throughout'.

Other words for persistence are toughness, obstinacy, stubbornness, bloody-mindedness and pig-headedness.

These words are not usually considered socially acceptable and some parents try to train such qualities out of their children, but the parent must allow the child to be stubborn when pursuing a constructive purpose. You wouldn't want to take away their body armour against life, would you?

Q: What is the greatest teacher?
A: Failure.

Thomas Edison was perhaps the biggest failure, that's if you were simply to count up the number of all his failed experiments. Yet out of them all, he obtained 1093 patents, the most ever gained by one person.

Edison invented the phonograph and the light bulb. Without him we might still be reading by gaslight. Learn from your failures. They are the stepping-stones to success.

Q: Which skill is central to all success?
A: Communication.

Communication is how we share ideas and interact with each other. Interestingly, the origin of the word communication is not chatting or yapping as you might expect; it comes from the Latin *co* meaning 'with' and *munia* or 'duty'. In other words, it seems we all have a natural duty to communicate with each other.

Q: Is there some quality that immediately sets a successful person apart?

A: Certainty.

Knowing that you know what you know is essential for success. It is also important to know when you don't know, because then you know to find out.

Q: What external factor most creates success?

A: Necessity.

Necessity is the mother of invention. A lot of people don't know that Mother Necessity once went on a date with that handsome rogue Assumption.

Q: Why didn't they become a couple?

A: Because Assumption is the father of Failure.

Q: Is there a part of success that is not immediately apparent?

A: Maybe honesty.

It might seem as though you don't need to be honest to succeed, and there seems to be many people who get rich by questionable and often illegal methods. But how successful are they really?

Success includes as a vital part of it the satisfaction of knowing what you have achieved.

So honesty is the best policy.

Q: How do successful people know where they are going?

A: Goals.

Everything starts with the goal or dream. A survey conducted in a US university discovered that only about 5% of the students set goals. When those same people were surveyed again many years later, it was discovered that the 5% who had set goals now accounted for 95% of the wealth of that class.

❓ Q: How big should my dreams be?
▪ A: Big.

Think big. Whatever game you are currently playing (because life is, after all, just a game) think bigger and both you and your life will grow bigger.

If you want some practice at thinking big, get hold of biographies of the great showman Phineas T. Barnum; his circus contemporaries James Bailey and the Ringling Brothers; the movie moguls who ran the original Hollywood film studios such as Sam Goldwyn, Darryl Zanuck and Adolph Zukor; and in the modern age, Richard Branson, Donald Trump and sporting greats such as Muhammad Ali.

❓ Q: What is absolutely paramount to being successful?
▪ A: Live by your own rules.

To be truly rich, a man must live
by his own values.
— *John Paul Getty*

One day, when she was a young child, the great ballerina Margot Fonteyn realised that there was no one exactly like her anywhere else in the world. She found it a very strange and empowering experience.

It is true. You are a unique individual.

The Great Gargoyle called Society tries to convince you otherwise. Governments, the media and the education system try to teach us that we are each a meaningless cog in some giant and very important machine. They just want us to be good little tax-payers.

You must cut the cloth of life to suit your own personality and make your own rules. This does not mean flouting the law or your duty to others, it simply means that in order to be successful you need to carve out your own niche in the world.

Be the star of your own life.

The Human Body

So, getting back to matters physical ... we started out with a little bit of sex and were just at the point of ecstasy. Now let's delve a little further into this instrument called the human body.

How are babies made?

A **Simon Sperm and Olive Ovum go on a date.**

Let's pick up again from the point when the sperm goes shooting out of the penis like an impatient driver who gets a green light.

Where is Simon Sperm off to? And who is with him? He is now heading for the womb in search of an unfertilised egg (called an ovum). And with him are five billion other little sperms, all shaped like tadpoles, wriggling like mad, running amok up the woman's vagina, charging forward like the barbarians invading Rome, all whooping and hollering, every one of them desperately in search of a date with the delectable Olive Ovum.

Q: What happens when sperm and ovum meet?
A: They merge and form a cell, the very first building block of what will be a brand new body.

Q: What is a cell?
A: A miniature oven.

A cell is a little energy production unit, smaller than a pinhead. It converts the energy that allows a body to move and function. The human body is made up of billions of such cells, most about one-hundredth of a millimetre wide, visible only through a microscope.

When a person puts on weight they're adding cells, and when they lose weight, they are losing cells. In other words, when you go on a diet you are murdering cells.

Q: How old are the cells?
A: The oldest is seven years old.

'But I am older than that!' you say. That's because the body replaces all its cells over a cycle of every seven years. That is definitely not the face you were born with!

The cells on the surface of our skin are continually being worn away and are replaced at a rate of about a million cells a day. Humans are just a bunch of biological litter louts.

Q: What is a skeleton?
A: A frame of lightweight rock.

The bones of the skeleton are made mainly from calcium, strengthened with a tough stringy material called collagen, similar to the way steel is used to reinforce concrete.

The spine is the first structure to form in the womb, and a baby is born with about 300 bones. Some of these fuse together as they grow so that an adult ends up with 206 separate bones.

The skeleton is also an internal suit of armour. Twelve pairs of ribs, along with the hip bones and spine, protect the internal organs of the heart, lungs, liver and intestines. The skull is a crash helmet and protects the brain. The spinal cord, which is the main highway of the nerves, runs through the middle of the spine and is protected by it.

? Q: What is the biggest bone in the human body?
A: The femur, or thighbone, which connects to the hip and the knee.

? Q: What are muscles?
A: Little mice running around under your skin.

Muscles are a system of internal ropes that move the body. They are made of stringy fibres banded together that pull and release by relaxing and contracting. They are essentially levers because most muscles are opposed by other muscles, and all muscles also pull against the skeleton.

The word 'muscle' comes from the Latin word for 'little mouse', *musculus*, as it was thought that when a person flexes their muscles it is like having mice running about under their skin. There are about 656 separate muscles in the human body, which make up about half the weight of a man and about one-third the weight of a woman.

? Q: How do the muscles and the bones get along with each other?
A: With flexible little diplomats in between.

These diplomats are connective tissue. Bones are hard stone and muscles are soft flesh, so the connective tissue is a hard but elasticated go-between. You might have come across connective tissue when eating meat. It was the gristle that you spat out.

? Q: What is fat?
A: Stored energy.

The body has to work hard to build muscle, but fat can be, and is, quickly stored as an oily substance under the skin. Originally, people would fatten up for the winter so that the body had some reserve energy for the days they could not find food. It was also to protect the body against the cold, since fat is an insulator.

These days it seems the only people who actually prefer to be fat are sumo wrestlers, or long-distance outdoor swimmers who need to keep their bodies warm in the cold water.

Q: How do people get fat today?
A: Eating unhealthy food.

Some people become overweight because they eat unhealthy food low in nutrients. The body demands a minimum amount of nutrients and tells them to keep eating until it has extracted sufficient nutrients. Since the food is low quality, more of it needs to be consumed resulting in eating excess carbohydrates that the body doesn't need and — unless they're working or exercising to use up the energy — converts into fat.

People also sometimes indulge in overeating simply out of habit or to make up for some lack in their lives.

Q: Why do we get hungry?
A: Because we run out of energy.

The cells — those tiny little taskmasters — start to get short of energy and send a grouchy message to the stomach which starts to grumble, telling you it's time to fill up.

Q: What does food consist of?
A: Generally, proteins, carbohydrates, fats, vitamins, minerals and water.

Q: Which ones provide the energy?
A: Proteins, carbohydrates and fats.

Proteins, such as eggs and meat, build muscle and repair injuries.

Carbohydrates, such as bread and rice, provide energy for activities. The word carbohydrate is made up from two of the key constituents of this form of energy: carbon and hydrogen.

Fats are a concentrated form of carbohydrate that come from animal products, plants, nuts and seeds.

❓ Q: So what do vitamins and minerals do?
A: They regulate special functions within the body.

Vitamin is from the Latin *vita* meaning 'life'. Vitamin C, for example, found in fresh fruit and vegetables, helps protect against disease.

Minerals are really rocks in very minute quantities. The mineral calcium, for example, forms teeth and bones, and is used for muscle function and for clotting blood.

❓ Q: Is water a food?
A: No, not really.

But water is vital to the functioning of a body. The body needs to be constantly refreshed with several litres of water a day. (On average, every glass of London tap water has previously passed through nine other people!)

❓ Q: So how does digestion work?
A: To food, your body is a wrecking machine.

Food has to be crushed down until it is small enough that it can be utilised by a tiny cell.

When you eat a ham and salad sandwich, the saliva in your mouth immediately starts to melt it down in your mouth while the teeth beat it up, chomping it and crushing it into small pieces.

That tasted nice! You swallow and think the job is done, but some of that food still has eight metres to go. We talk about 'letting our food go down' but it is not gravity which drags it down; muscles push it down a tube into your stomach.

Your stomach is the main warehouse. As soon as the poor, bedraggled food arrives it is mugged by burning stomach acid. Then the stomach walls move in on it and try to crush it like in that *Star Wars* film.

In the movies, the heroes usually get away, but not your food. It has now been reduced to a mushy, unrecognisable pulp.

43

But there is more to come as it gets pushed through the long and twisting maze of the small intestine. All the time, the food is getting dizzier and smaller and smaller until at last the particles are small enough to pass through the small channels of the wall of the intestine into the bloodstream.

❓ Q: Who's got the biggest appetite?

A: Probably Mr Eat Everything.

He is a Frenchman known as Monsieur Mangetout (*mange* meaning 'eat', and *tout* or 'everything') who can eat glass and metal and has even eaten a whole Cessna 150 light aircraft.

❓ Q: Where does the waste material go?

A: Ah yes, the yucky bit.

Anything which is not digested gets pushed on into the large intestine, which removes the water from the bladder and any remaining um ... solid waste is excreted through the rectum. Everybody is familiar with this process and knows many rude names for it!

Apparently it takes about 15 hours (though this may vary) for food that will be waste material to pass right through the body.

❓ Q: Why do we burp?

A: This is a release of gas from the stomach rising upwards.

❓ Q: Why do we fart?

A: This is a release of gas from the intestines downwards.

This particular subject is of great amusement to small children and also goes by many names, including dropping one, doing a whizzbang and letting one off. The best fuel to provide these fun fireworks are beans and cabbage.

? Q: Why do farts smell?
A: So they can be appreciated by deaf people.

That's a joke, by the way.

? Q. What is the correct diet?
A. Nobody has really worked out the correct diet for the human body.

There are many points of view on this, and even more food fads, but basically a person should have a balanced diet, which means the right mix of protein, carbohydrates, vitamins and so on. This will differ as people have different bodies and different tastes.

The fresher and less processed food is, the more nutrition there is in it.

? Q: How do you lose weight?
A: Increase outflow, decrease inflow.

Eat healthier, exercise more and gradually decrease the junk food.

Another good tip to note is that cells keep asking for fuel until they get it. This means the stomach might continue demanding food for up to an hour after someone who was hungry has eaten, simply because the cells have not received the fuel yet. That causes many people to overeat at a meal, thinking they are still hungry.

When a body needs energy, it takes it from the nearest available source, so the part of the body that you exercise is the part that will lose weight.

? Q: How does the food get to the cell?
A: Through the bloodstream.

The bloodstream is the transport system of the body. The blood carries the nutrients from the digestive system and oxygen from the lungs, and carries away waste materials from cells.

This whole traffic system is driven by the heart, which is a muscular pump about the size of a clenched fist. If you open and clench your fist, you will get a rough idea how it works.

The heart beats around 60 to 80 times a minute. This is slow compared with a hedgehog's heart, which beats 300 times a minute.

The human heart beats about 40 million times a year or about 3 billion times a lifetime, without taking a day off or getting paid any overtime.

All it asks in return is that you stay fit and healthy.

Q: What are the lungs?
A: A pair of bellows.

Cells need fuel, oxygen and water to perform their chemical reactions. The lungs draw in air from outside the body, retain the oxygen and breathe the waste product of carbon dioxide back out into the air.

Plants need carbon dioxide to produce their own food, so everybody is sweet.

The lungs have about 2600 km (1615 miles) of airways. If you could spread out the network of one person's lungs over the ground, they would cover a tennis court.

Q: Why do we spit?
A: To clear the mouth, throat and lungs.

For example, vigorous exercise causes the airways of the lungs to get worked, forcing up unwanted material which when mixed with saliva in the mouth can be ejected by spitting.

Q: Why do we sneeze?
A: Emergency ejection from the lungs.

A woman from Worcestershire once sneezed every day for 977 days. That's a lot of gazumptites!

? Q: What are the nerves?
A: The body's postal service.

Nerves are a little faster than the post, probably closer to the speed of email since the speed of nerve waves is about 10 feet (3 m) a second. It has to be, because when your body touches a hot poker, you have to know about it *fast*. Ouch!

? Q: What is hair?
A: A natural form of clothing.

Hair warms and protects. So much of it grows on top of your head because 50% of heat escapes through the head (tough luck if you are bald — wear a cap). Eyebrows prevent sweat from dripping into the eyes and hairs in the nostrils act as guards against pollutants.

Both hair and nails are made from a protein called keratin, which also produces the scales of reptiles and the feathers of birds.

Traffic wardens do not have hair under their uniforms. They have scales.

? Q: Why do I always seem to be cutting my fingernails and toenails at different times?
A: Because fingernails grow quicker than toenails.

? Q: What is the head?
A: Communication central of the body.

There are a bunch of holes in the head out of which peep the major perception channels. They are sight, hearing, taste and smell. The fifth, touch, covers the whole body. These perceptions all monitor contact with the physical world by registering physical particles.

Our sense of touch monitors the most solid particles (have you ever walked into a door?).

The next biggest particle size is taste, which deals with food, such as chewing a jam donut.

Then there is smell, caused by the release of small particles into the atmosphere, such as manure, which gets right up your nose.

Then you are into the particles of smaller wavelengths (although sometimes sound can feel quite solid, especially if you have ever been to a rock concert!).

Sight depends on detecting the smallest particles, which are so small that light moves at almost 186,000 miles (300,000 km) per second (except on its day off).

Q: What is a face?
A: The best cartoon ever created.

The face is a moving message board, conveying communications through expression.

Q: What is physical beauty?
A: Just an idea, actually.

There have been so many ideas of beauty in ages past. In Europe during the Middle Ages, a woman was supposed to be pear-shaped.

There are some tribes in South America whose members mutilate their ears to make themselves more beautiful. A few African and Asian cultures consider a woman's beauty to be judged by how many rings she wears under her neck (the neck muscles become so dependent on these that the neck can collapse if they are taken away).

This practice actually started long ago to try and make women *ugly* to slave traders who were stealing them away. In time, what was considered to be ugliness slowly evolved into its exact opposite: beauty.

So beauty is just an idea.

Q: What is plastic surgery?
A: Changing your appearance through a medical procedure.

Q: So can plastic surgery help people?
A: Only if you believe that beauty is skin deep.

Virtually 100% of the people I have seen interviewed on the subject say they undergo plastic surgery to increase their confidence.

Italian and Hindu surgeons had been practising plastic surgery for several hundred years before the mechanised killing of the twentieth century forced rapid advances in the field.

One of the great pioneers of modern plastic surgery was New Zealander Archibald McIndoe, who formed the Guinea Pig Club at Queen Victoria Cottage Hospital in East Grinstead, Sussex, during the Second World War. The title came out of the sardonic humour of the young fighter pilots, whose faces McIndoe was repairing. They reckoned they were his 'guinea pigs'.

These had once been handsome young men. Now they looked more like fairground freaks. The devastation often caused marriages to end and engagements to be broken off. In one case, a young man's fiancée told him that how he now looked made no difference to her personal feelings, but the man summarily ended their engagement himself.

McIndoe was a great man who knew to treat the spirit as well as the body. He kept a piano and a gramophone in his wards. Men were allowed to put pin-ups on the walls and McIndoe selected nurses who were cheerful. He allowed the men to keep whisky and beer under their beds. His reasoning was that there was no point making new faces unless the men had reason to smile.

One day the man who had broken his engagement — and who now had what was a passable imitation of a face — walked into a shop to find his former fiancée standing in front of him. Grabbing him she told him, 'You got away from me once, you're not going to do it again.'

Q: Come on, looks are important, aren't they?
A: Nah, not really.

Bully Hayes was an American adventurer who ended up in Arrowtown, New Zealand during the gold rush in 1860, where he opened a hotel. His problem was getting enough barmaids to go round. Women were scarcer than gold and probably a whole lot more valuable. As soon as the hotel had a good barmaid, a miner would steal her away to be married.

In the end, Hayes resorted to the brilliant idea of advertising for the ugliest barmaids he could find. But that didn't work either. The miners kept snapping them up anyway.

They wanted a companion, not an ornament.

Q: What is beauty?
A: Beauty is in the eye of the beholder.

But before it is in the eye of the beholder, it must be in the heart of the one who is being beheld.

Q: What exactly is a body?
A: It's a mobile engine.

The body is the temple of the soul.

If it really is just a vehicle, then who is the driver?

Chapter 2
Relationships, Dating and Love

Most people seem to live their lives in small orbits of friendliness. Relationships can be rewarding and yet sometimes so fraught with difficulties. And then there's romance!

Family

What is a family?

A **The basic building block of society.**

The family is the smallest self-perpetuating group in a society.

Traditional farming communities depended on the family unit to be its labour force; therefore a single person was considered detrimental to the economic structure of the time, unless you were somehow made part of the family unit.

The basic family unit of parents and children is known as a nuclear family — but not because it blows up every time there's an argument about who does the washing up.

Q: What is the first rule of family?
A: A family that eats and plays together, stays together.

As a comparison, the word 'companion' comes from the French *com* meaning 'with' and *pain* or 'bread'; someone you eat bread with.

Q: Why do families fight?
A: Violation of moral codes.

Any relationship or group forms its own moral code. These are agreements that are held between them, some that are openly stated and others not. Even pirates had moral codes, such as 'Men caught stealing will have their noses slit and will be marooned on a desert island' or 'Any fool trying to smuggle his wife aboard disguised as a man will be put to death immediately.'

Conflicts occur when a person violates the agreement, and communication breaks down.

Q: What is the solution to this?
A: Honesty and communication.

Honesty and trust are the basis of all human relations, but even more important is communication. If whales can communicate with each other over a distance of a thousand kilometres, then people should be able to manage it over a matter of a few metres.

Q: Is there a release valve to reduce tensions?
A: Family games.

Playing games are ways that a family can argue and fight, but in a constructive way instead of a destructive way.

In romantic relationships, sex can be a good release valve, especially as people generally don't talk during it and therefore can't argue. Anyway, sex is just a form of wrestling.

Q: How do you choose your friends?
A: By their actions.

Do their words match their actions? If so, and their actions are constructive, that friendship will last and be beneficial.

Q: What is love?
A: The expression of intense affinity.

Nepalese women demonstrate their love for their husbands by washing their men's feet and drinking the dirty water.

Women are capable of incredibly deep and powerful love. If you are a man, never underestimate how much your woman loves you.

Even stronger is a woman's love for her children.

Stronger still is a child's love for his or her parents.

Q: How do I meet my soul mate?
A: There is a very good trick to this, actually.

And it is a necessary one too, since some people select their romantic partner with less caution than they would use to buy a second-hand washing machine. You at least want to know that the pump is working.

The trick is to write a shopping list of all the qualities you think they should possess. But don't expect perfection — a 90% hit rate is acceptable.

A friend wrote a list of 20 attributes and is now happily married to a man who had 19 of them. What was the one she missed out on?

He doesn't dance.

? Q: So where do I meet them?
■ A: Circulate.

Just work out where the type of person would hang out and go there. Or what type of clubs they would belong to and join them.

? Q: What are some good chat-up lines?
■ A: How about 'Hello'?

A man sees an attractive girl in the street and says to her, 'Thank you.' She says, 'What for?' and he says, 'For being so beautiful.'

Or

'Thank you for decorating the day with your beauty.'

Or

'I just want to say it is my duty to admire your beauty.'

? Q: How about chat-up lines from a girl to a guy?
■ A: 'Hello.' With a smile.

If she is feeling daring, 'Excuse me, I was just wondering if your personality matched your thighs.'

Or if she is feeling very daring, 'What is the biggest organ on your body?' And as he hesitates with shock or embarrassment, she quickly adds, 'It's your skin.'

? Q: What's the next step?
■ A: Check availability.

This does not mean when they are free to go on a date, but whether they already have a partner. The fast way to do this is to say something like, 'Are you married?'

For which you might get the fast answer, 'Unfortunately for you, I am.'

The slower and more enjoyable route is 'going fishing'. You engage them in friendly conversation that ultimately elicits whether or not they have a partner.

The upside of this technique is that though (if they have one) you might lose a lover, you might gain a friend.

If they are a bit slow supplying the needed information, you can always throw in a little prompt like, 'Oh, what does your partner think of that?'

And they say, 'I haven't got one.'

And you think *bingo!*

Q: Anyway, you meet them for the first time and they are available. What's next?
A: Get their contact details.

If they write them down, just make sure you can read them, because the hand that is smitten by love is sometimes a little shaky.

Q: And then?
A: Arrange the first date, of course.

Tell them you will take them to the zoo as you know they will feel comfortable in the company of their relatives.

No seriously, just find something you both like to do and do that.

DO NOT try to impress them on the first date. People see through all that bunk.

Just be natural. If you naturally knock over tables and dip your tie in the soup, just do that.

Q: Is there a tip that really works well on the first date?
A: Listening.

Listening is a very underrated skill. Everybody likes to be listened to.

Q: What if I realise they are not for me?
A: Tell them straight away, honestly and politely.

You also have to give them a reason they can understand, but of course not a negative one like, 'You have a pimple on your nose.'

Q: What if you are not sure?
A: Ask for another date.

Q: What about the fear of rejection?
A: Fear, like beauty, exists only in the mind.

Can you take fear and boil it in a saucepan? Can you wallpaper your bedroom with fear? When you take action, by communication or deed, fear just evaporates.

And do not fall into the trap of thinking the other person is perfect. We are all escapees from a Dickens novel.

Q: Okay, so we go out on a few dates. When do we have sex?
A: I knew you'd get back to that.

You should have sex when you are both comfortable having sex.

Q: So the first sexual approach is the kiss?
A: Actually, before that comes flirting.

The kiss is usually the first sexual *contact*.

Q: What is flirting?
A: Flirting is play sex.

Flirting is all show and no commitment. It is the gorilla beating his chest. It is the bird doing a crazy little dance and making strange noises. In human terms it is part-banter, part-dance, with no real commitment yet, rather like the dance that the two boxers go through before they actually throw any punches.

The word 'flirt' is imitative of the basic, physical action of flirting, meaning 'to move or throw with a jerk'.

❓ Q: What's the best way to flirt?
A: In a spirit of fun.

Try flirting with humorous, playful jokes that are centred around relationships, love, romance and sex, encouraging and taunting the other person in a gentle way.

❓ Q: Then the kiss?
A: Before that you have to close down the distance.

In normal human relations, people maintain an invisible space around them, similar to ballroom dancing, where each dancer has a defined space within the discipline of the dance.

As romance develops between two people, these invisible spaces start to overlap and merge.

You cross the border into their personal space and when they don't stop you and ask you for your passport, you know you are getting somewhere.

Then magically your heads move closer and you realise that your mouth is starting to angle towards their mouth.

For a moment, you are walking the tightrope between acceptance and rejection.

Then you kiss them and either they kiss you back or you get a slap on the face.

❓ Q: What if you think they might be 'the one'?
A: Ah, there is an ancient, lost technology called courtship.

Courtship often took a long time and this was because it was meant to be long and involved enough to ensure the marriage lasted at least as long as it took for the children to grow up.

In the Victorian era, ladies were not even supposed to place books by male and female authors next to each other on bookshelves, unless the authors of those books were married.

Things are more casual today, but the old-fashioned method actually works. You should still go through a testing and bonding process.

❓ Q: What is the purpose of marriage?
A: To keep people together.

In the marriage ceremony, private promises are made to each other in public. That makes them harder to break. Symbols such as rings are used to bind each other together.

Marriage is actually a legal contract: it's hard to get out of, so you should make sure that all your ducks are in a row before you get into one.

❓ Q: Do you have to get married?
A: Not necessarily, these days.

> *They are our enemies, we marry them.*
> — Nuer proverb

The women of ancient Greece used to count their age from the day they were married, because it was thought that their lives only began at that point.

Today, marriage is intended to symbolise a sound relationship. You can have a sound relationship without getting married.

You can also get married and have an unsound relationship.

Having a sound relationship is the key.

Q: What are the disadvantages of getting married?
A: The cost of the ceremony.

If you have to pay for it yourself, you'd be better off spending the money on a deposit on a house.

Really, people should reduce the costs of their wedding by selling tickets to family and friends.

They could even hold a raffle. The traditional custom is that whoever gets to catch the bride's bouquet gets married next.

Q: What are the advantages of getting married?
A: A bit more certainty.

Plus the woman gets a new name (if she wants one). If there are children, the whole family can end up with the same surname.

Q: Is there anything you have to do before you get married?
A: Make sure you have the same goals.

Years ago a man just wanted a woman who knew how to milk a cow.

People's lives are so much more varied these days and there are so many different goals. Both parties should at least have the same goals for the relationship.

Q: Anything else?
A: They should agree how to disagree.

They should sort out basic agreements and systems, including how to let off steam and how to handle disagreements.

Once there was a couple who had a fierce argument during a game of cards and so resolved never to play cards with each other again. After 20 years of married bliss, they were driving home from a party one night and commented on how they never argued. They remembered the decision they had made after the game of cards, began discussing the reasons for the argument, and by the time they got home they were not speaking to each other.

Q: Anything else before I propose?
A: You both have to agree to keep working at the relationship.

Only in fairy tales do things end happily ever after. Cinderella did not have glass slippers. They were originally fur. That got changed later by a translator.

Nor did the frog turn into a handsome prince because of a kiss. In the original, the frog was thrown against a wall. Splat! Very violent.

Love is just the ice cream. For a relationship to succeed takes creativity and hard work.

Q: How do I propose to a woman?
A: Get down on one knee and give her a ring.

If she doesn't answer the phone, go around and see her.

Q: Can women propose marriage?
A: Traditionally they can in a leap year.

Outside of a leap year they should give subtle (and not so subtle) hints.

Q: Why is the best man called the best man?
A: Because he's the best kidnapper.

Best man was a Scottish term from the days when they kidnapped their future brides. The one in the group who was best kidnapper was called the 'best man'.

❓ Q: Why do brides carry bouquets?
■ A: Because they stink.

The Romans loved to take baths. After the fall of the Roman Empire, people did everything the opposite, so the Romans bathed only once a year. They had the annual bath in May and by June, which was when most marriages took place, they were starting to whiff a bit. Hence the bouquet.

So next time you go to a wedding, sidle up to the bride and whisper, 'I know why you are holding that bouquet ...'

❓ Q: Is it necessary to be faithful?
■ A: Absolutely.

We live in a monogamous culture, the word coming from the Greek *mono* meaning 'one' and *gamous* or 'marriage; married to one person at a time'.

Though to make them feel at home, Inuit men used to lend guests their wives.

But don't be a two-timing love rat like the male pied flycatcher, which will often keep separate nests several kilometres apart. If both females hatch their eggs, he will desert one of them.

Just because a 1631 edition of the Bible accidentally left the words *and not* out of *thou shalt not commit adultery* is no reason to play around. Nor do you want to suffer an early French punishment for adultery: chasing a chicken through town naked.

Everyone wants a relationship where they can fully trust the other person.

Q: What if I did have a moment of weakness?
A: 'Fess up and make amends.

There was once a millionaire who ran off with his secretary for six weeks, realised what an error he had made, went back to his wife and told her the truth. He asked what she wanted to make up for the damage he had caused. She asked for a horse from the Spanish Riding School in Vienna. He provided it and they have been happily married ever since.

Q: Why do people get divorced?
A: Because of a reverse of the above.

They stop communicating so that lots of unsaids and resentments build up.

In Anglo-Saxon times, a man could divorce his wife on the grounds that she was too passionate!

Q: What is the secret to a long and happy marriage?
A: Responsibility and caring for the other person.

Q: Is there one piece of relationship advice that ranks above all others?
A: Communicate!

Children

The natural result of a relationship is often children — those cheeky-cheerfuls who bruise silence and make magic out of motion. They are both a delight and annoying little pests.

If you are not a parent maybe you have not asked these questions yet. But then again, you were a child once (or have you forgotten?).

What is a child?

A   One word sums it up: pestertainment.

A very good teacher once said to me, 'A child is a little person.'

They are not objects. They are not possessions. They have rights like adults.

Q: When does childhood end?
A: When the child becomes independent.

The law decides that there is a specific age of legal entitlement for every single person. But people are different. Jack Daniels of whisky fame bought his distillery when he was 13 years old. He got his parents to sign the papers.

Q: What is the first and most important thing to give children?
A: Stability.

A child needs: a home, tolerant and understanding parents, possessions they can call their own, some space they can call their own, some creativity they can call their own, lots of friends and activities.

❓ Q: How do you treat children?
■ **A: Treat them the way you want them to be.**

An example of this took place in New Zealand during the nineteenth century. A young white child was kidnapped by the indigenous Maori people and lived with them for two years. When the child was finally recaptured, he was found to be very high-spirited and aggressive, which was because the traditional Maori style of upbringing instilled a warrior spirit in their children.

I have noticed that children who are treated like criminals (always being investigated by their parents) and told that they are naughty, lo and behold tend to be naughty. And they have the potential to be criminals.

I have also noticed that children who are addressed in an intelligent and civilised manner tend to respond in an intelligent and civilised manner.

Treat and talk to children with respect, dignity, positivity and intelligence and you will get respectful, dignified, positive, intelligent children.

❓ Q: Are there any underlying attitudes I should have towards children?
A: Yes, three attitudes.

◇ They are very valuable people.

◇ Nothing is impossible.

◇ They are allowed to reject anything they don't agree with.

❓ Q: What is the best type of upbringing for a child?
■ **A: Tending towards the liberal.**

A high proportion of very successful people are often brought up by or have spent a lot of time with their grandparents. Grandparents have often mellowed with age and don't issue a lot of orders and give children the space to grow and flourish.

? Q: How do I get children to behave?
■ A: Use the old Native American trick.

No, this does not mean tie them to a totem pole and dance around them threateningly waving a tomahawk. So-called Indian 'savages' were actually very civilised and had very well-behaved children. This was because all the adults in the tribe were in a conspiracy against the children.

A child would be heading towards the river to commit some terribly naughty crime and another adult, not part of his immediate family, would stop him and say, 'What a good boy you are, going to get water for your mother.'

The child would stop dead in his tracks, somewhat confused, because he *had* been about to do something really bad.

The tribe kept this up all the time, continually encouraging positive behaviour in the child.

? Q: Why do children misbehave?
■ A: Because they are bored.

I learned from a very early age that it was important for us kids to help provide for the home, to be contributors rather than just takers.
— Sam Walton

If there is no constructive game to play, children will end up creating a destructive one.

In Singapore there is a child prodigy called Ainan who, when he goes to the beach, often writes complex chemical equations in the sand. His mother was asked if he ever misbehaves. She replied, 'Yes, when not fulfilled, but when he's really into something he will light up like a light bulb.'

Work is really just a game — the difference is that something is being produced that is valuable to another.

Little children love to volunteer for work. It makes them feel valuable.

65

They will almost fight you to be allowed to carry your shopping bag even though it may be so heavy that they can barely drag it along the floor.

So let them. Which is more important — the eggs or the child?

? Q: Who sets a child's goals?
■ A: The child.

When he was younger, American actor Adam Sandler told his aunt he wanted to be a comedian. She said she thought it would better if he became a doctor. But he insisted he wanted to be a comedian, so she said, 'Why don't you become a funny doctor?'

It is up to the child to set up the goal. It is up to the family simply to support and encourage it, even if it does turn the parents into unpaid taxi drivers.

When he was a young boy, All Black Dan Carter used to kick his rugby ball on to his parents' roof. They could have shouted at him. Instead they built a set of rugby posts down the bottom of their garden.

Now he is acknowledged as one of the best kickers in the world.

? Q: Are children always demanding of attention?
■ A: Actually ... there's a really good trick for that.

I worked it out and then I read that the film director Steven Spielberg, who has a large family, does a similar thing. It's very useful if you tend to work long hours.

The trick is that you *totally ignore your children*, let them get on with what they are doing and you get on with what you are doing.

Then, suddenly, they come bowling into your study demanding your FULL ATTENTION. They want to play a game with you or show you something. So you end off what you are doing. If you say, 'Give me a few minutes to finish this and I will be right with you,' they will. They are very civilised.

Then you give them your FULL ATTENTION. After a while they are happy as Larry and tootle off to their next game.

You go back to what you were doing and everybody is happy.

❓ Q: How do you best answer a child's questions?
A: Truthfully, but succinctly.

Children prefer dialogues to monologues. If they want more information, they'll simply ask another question. They will keep asking until they've got the answer they want.

It has been estimated that a four-year-old will ask up to 400 'Why?' questions a day. But that's just an estimate. Whenever I ask parents or grandparents how many questions they answer, the reply is always the same, 'Thousands!'

❓ Q: What if you don't know the answer?
A: Tell them you don't know the answer.

Then help them find the answer.

❓ Q: How do you teach children to be successful?
A: By encouraging them to persist.

Don't get into the lackadaisical attitude of, 'Don't worry about it; it doesn't matter. Leave it.' Gently help and encourage them to carry every task through to completion.

❓ Q: When should you start allowing children to lead?
A: At every opportunity.

If you go to the zoo, let them commandeer the guide map and lead. And let them do it. Don't keep double guessing them ('That's not an elephant, dear. Elephants have a trunk and that animal only has a suitcase').

Let them give orders. There are few sights as amusing as a young child

waiting at the junction for his parents and shouting grumpily back at them, 'Come on, hurry up!'

Q: How do children learn?
A: At first, by absorbing their environment.

A child begins life as a blank slate. As they gain information, they compare the existing information with new information. That is why children sometimes say the funniest things, such as, 'A butterfly is a piece of a cloud that has fallen out of the sky.'

Children also learn by imitation, like the young boy who, after riding as a passenger in his father's car, drove around the garden in his kiddie car, shouting at all the flowers 'Idiot! Imbecile!'

Q: What is the best weapon to arm a child with?
A: Vocabulary.

This helps children understand and identify the world around them.

Everyone knows the teaching game of pointing out parts of the body and telling the child what they are: 'These are the eyes, this is the nose ...' This game can be extended to include almost anything, including the house, the flowers in the garden, the tools in the tool shed and further afield. This will also give the child more certainty and confidence.

Q: Are nursery rhymes still useful?
A: Yes.

Rhymes allow children to practise verbal skills. The action of reciting and singing means that sounds have to be hit more clearly (rather like running instead of walking). Also the child absorbs rhythms that they can use later in life. The great actor Marlon Brando once said that his mother sang him thousands of songs when he was a child.

Q: How fast does vocabulary develop?
A: Once a child starts talking, they don't stop.

As you know, the first word takes about a year to learn and is usually either 'mum' or 'dad', and both parents will argue about which one the mumbled articulation is. The following advance in vocabulary by age is very approximate and will obviously vary from child to child.

Age	Words	Age	Words
1 year	1	3 years	1000
18 months	18	5 to 6 years	3000
2 years	200 to 300		

But don't sweat the action. Children learn different things at different rates, and generally seem to catch up with each other. Some reports say Albert Einstein couldn't speak until he was seven.

Q: What are toys?
A: Objects with which to practise life skills.

Childish play actually has a purpose as practise for real-life situations, the same way fox cubs will practice hunting skills on each other. Though these days, it could be argued that toys and games have become more of an entertainment; do they teach the child a skill or simply turn them into spectators?

Q: What are puzzles?
A: The intermediary step between toys and books.

Q: What is the best way for a child to learn?
A: By playing games.

A child's primary goals are to have adventure and fun and to grow up. And if their learning is framed or supported around games, they will learn. The original meaning of the word 'study' in Greek is 'eager'. Socrates said, 'To instruct we must first entertain.' Unless people are actually enjoying their learning, they're not really learning.

Q: Is there a cunning little trick to help children learn?
A: Test them.

Children love to be tested in a fun way.

Q: Should a family member start teaching a small child to read?
A: Certainly, if both child and adult want to.

A great many successful people have been tutored by a family member at an early age.

The derivation of the word 'tutor' is someone who watches over you. Oprah Winfrey was tutored by her grandmother, Hattie May. There was no television, and so reading became a pleasure for her. She could do arithmetic, read and write by the time she was three.

A parent should certainly be more than a babysitter, as a child is a sponge for knowledge. An English-speaking child in a foreign country will pick up the new language at a speed that makes their parents seem very *duh*.

Q: What is the best method to teach children to read?
A: By learning the sounds of the letters.

Like dieting, over the years, the simple subject of reading has become subject to a host of fads.

Language developed as a sound code. The word language comes from *lingua* which means 'tongue'. The first spoken words were actually just copies of existing sounds. For example, we say that a wolf howls. Though we spell them quite differently today, the words 'wolf' and 'howl' are both a written representation of the sound a wolf makes.

Words, therefore, developed through this system and should be taught by this system, which is otherwise known as phonics or 'The cat sat on the mat' method. The child learns how to sound each of the sounds and that way, when confronted with an enormous word such as 'hippopotamus', all they have to do is to sound it out.

? Q: So, is there an easy, practical way of teaching them how to read?

A: A little bit at a time.

First, you read children stories. They will follow the pages, but without being able to read the words. Start pointing out letters and getting them to identify that letter in other locations on the page.

Next, get them to blend letters together, and then a whole word.

As you continue to read them stories, encourage the child to read short phrases of easy words such as 'The cat sat on the mat.'

Then move to whole sentences. You will eventually reach a stage where you and the child may be reading alternate sentences or alternate pages.

As you are reading your page, the child will probably follow it silently with you, so a good trick is to deliberately change the words, often humorously. The child will immediately stop you and correct you, which is good fun for both of you.

Finally, of course, the roles will be reversed and one night, the child will read the whole story to *you*.

Does your child have the potential to be a genius? What about you? Do you have the potential to be a genius?

Children are so smart and come out with such ingenious solutions to problems, that I suspect they are already geniuses and that as they get older, we train it out of them.

Genius

What is a genius?

A An exceptionally talented individual.

We usually think of a genius as someone who can solve a mathematical problem by instantly reeling off a whole screed of numbers correctly. The Oxford Dictionary describes genius as someone who has 'exceptional intellectual or creative power or other natural ability'.

In ancient Rome, a genius was a personal guardian spirit that was worshipped. Every person was born with one, who protected and guided them through their life. On their birthday, presents were actually given to the genius. Then when they died, their family honoured the genius. Today, we still revere genius but in different way.

Q: Are geniuses born?
A: Yes and no.

There are some child geniuses whose abilities seem to appear out of nowhere. Mozart was one. He never went to school and started composing his own music at the age of five.

Mathematical genius Alexander Aitken was born in Dunedin, New Zealand on April Fool's Day, 1895. But Alex was no fool. He was once asked to multiply 987,654,321 by 123,456,789 in his head. Why don't you try it? Got the answer yet? It took Aitken half a minute to work it out. Of course the answer is 121,932,631,112,635,269. Easy peasy.

Aitken said he broke the answers down into their elements and that the numbers almost played a tune to him. For one calculation, he divided the numbers into five and submitted them to a German waltz tune.

But Aitken was not a child prodigy. He found arithmetic boring at school. Then when he was nearly 14 years old, he had a very good maths teacher and one day maths suddenly snapped into focus and he became fascinated by numbers. Later, after the first calculators were invented, however, Aitken noticed his calculating abilities deteriorated since he could see there was less use for them.

So genius is not necessarily present at birth, nor an absolute state.

? Q: What's one of the most noticeable features of geniuses?
A: They are curious.

Albert Einstein said the important thing is not to stop questioning. Curiosity is an almost insatiable desire to know. It is a very powerful force.

Alexander Graham Bell is famous as the inventor of the telephone. But he invented many other things and was co-founder of the National Geographic Society, which publishes *National Geographic* magazine. Against his will — he had too many experiments he wanted to do — Bell was forced to take over as president in 1898 when the society only had about 1000 members. By 1912, under his stewardship, it grew to over 100,000 members.

He described curiosity thus: 'My mind concentrates itself on the subject that happens to occupy it and then all things else in the universe, including father, mother, wife, children, *life itself*, becomes for the time being of secondary importance.'

❓ Q: What else is noticeable about geniuses?
◾ A: They are very imaginative.

The power of imagination is far, far more important than knowledge. Knowledge consists merely of existing ideas. Only imagination can create new ones.

Nikola Tesla (1856–1943) was one of the great pioneers of electricity. He discovered alternating current, running the concept in his head for several years to work out the flaws. Then one day, as Tesla was walking though the park with his friend, he finally visualised the complete solution. He was surprised that his friend could not see it all because Tesla could see it standing in front of him in three dimensions.

❓ Q: Are curiosity and imagination enough?
◾ A: No, you have to be persistent.

American inventor Charles Kettering said an inventor fails 999 times and is happy to succeed once. Winston Churchill said that life consists of moving from defeat to defeat with no loss of enthusiasm.

He also said, 'Never, ever, ever, ever give up.'

❓ Q: But geniuses are normal, aren't they?
◾ A: No, the truth is that they are a little bit crazy.

That's because the level of their creative thinking is above the level of analytical thinking that most people use in their day-to-day lives.

As a child Thomas Edison demonstrated a great curiosity. He was even a little wacky; he once lay on goose eggs to see if he could hatch them. Another time he persuaded a friend to drink a medicine that made water fizzy. His theory was that his friend would fill up with bubbles and float through the air. When Edison took his strange and original ideas to school, his teacher thought he was either backward or insane. When his mother discovered this, she took him out of school and home-schooled him.

Good job she did.

❓ Q: Are geniuses eccentric?
A: Yes, they think outside the box.

In his autobiography *Work in Progress*, Michael Eisner describes the 'Gong Shows' that he introduced when he became chief executive of Disney Studios. These were business meetings where people were encouraged to put forward the craziest ideas on the basis that most of them would be gonged, but a few excellent ones would get through. This was based on Eisner's philosophy that only when people were sufficiently free of inhibition did they start to think imaginatively.

When Eisner was originally put forward for the chief executive position, conservative members of the board at Disney had been unsure of his appointment because of his creative tendencies. But Stanley Gold, a business partner of Roy Disney, nephew of Walt Disney, lent his support for Eisner, saying that every great film studio had been run by 'the crazies' including Walt Disney himself.

❓ Q: But surely, it's more serious than that?
A: Who gave you the idea that seriousness and creativity go together?

Benjamin Franklin is one of the great men of American history. The US was built out of four great documents: The Declaration of Independence, the Treaty of Alliance with France, the Treaty of Peace with Great Britain and the Constitution of the United States. Franklin's is the only signature on all four of those documents.

Thomas Jefferson described him as 'the greatest man and ornament of the age'. Americans still revere Franklin. He's on the $100 note.

Among other things, Franklin was an electrical pioneer. One Christmas he planned to impress his friends by killing the turkey using electricity. He had rigged up some primitive batteries to provide the power, but became overconfident and as he was talking to one of his guests, he brushed against one of the batteries.

There was a flash, a loud bang and Franklin was sent flying across the room.

After he had dusted himself off, Franklin became quite intrigued by this. It reminded him of lightning. This led to him proving that lightning was electricity and inventing the lightning rod. This discovery was very valuable because in France, for example, 103 bell ringers were killed between 1753 and 1786 as a result of lightning striking church towers.

Q: What sort of upbringing do geniuses tend to have?
A: Free and creative.

Bill Hamilton is best known for inventing the Hamilton jet boat, a flat-bottomed boat that could navigate very shallow rivers. He grew up on a large farm in the South Island of New Zealand. His mother had read that children should not have formal education until the age of seven, so during that time Hamilton lived a Huckleberry Finn sort of existence, following his curiosity and sense of adventure, returning home only when driven there by hunger.

He also conducted all manner of bizarre experiments, once collecting sea water in a bottle only to discover when he got it home that for some reason the tide no longer worked.

Another time, he tried to recreate the effects of the twisting ride of a scenic railway he had seen at an exhibition by tying four ropes to four corners of a box and then tying the other ends to a tree. He got into the box, twisted the ropes tight and then let go. His experiment created such centrifugal force that he was trapped inside this whirling dervish for a while until he staggered out to crawl away and be sick.

Q: Are all geniuses thinkers?
A: No, many are people of action.

The great explorers that pioneered the geographical discovery of the Earth were generally rogues, madmen and wild men. They were the film stars in the days before there was film.

One of them was Richard Burton, who discovered the source of the Nile River in 1858. He was half-pirate, half-poet, an English gentleman adventurer descended from the gypsies. He was a man who did not so much live life as explode through it. He attended Oxford University but was thrown out of it for going to horse races (his other hobby was challenging students to duels). He was a scientist and a linguist (learning 25 languages and translating many foreign classics — including the *Kama Sutra* and other erotic works, which offended the prudish Victorians).

The men who sailed the great oceans were of a similar ilk. When Christopher Columbus went in search of the Spice Islands (but instead bumped into a big chunk of land that became known as America), many expected he would sail off the edge of the world. In those days many mariners could not swim. When one ship went down, the crew tied a rope to a pig on board, held on to the rope and the pig dragged them to safety.

Q: Apart from being crazy, is there anything else odd about geniuses?

A: A lot of them were sick as children.

This kept coming up so frequently in my research that for a while it completely flummoxed me. How could sickness have anything to do with genius? It took me a while to work it out.

Take Irving Thalberg. He was sickly as a child, but was running Universal Pictures by the age of 21. What happened was that Thalberg's neighbour owned a studio; one day they got into conversation and Thalberg displayed such an extensive knowledge of what constituted a good story that he was immediately employed. Thalberg's knowledge came about because he had read many of the great classics of literature. He had read them when he was sick as a child.

Edison was also sickly as a child, and was mainly home-schooled by his mother.

So there's the point. Unfortunately, being sick is one of the few ways you can get out of school. And what do you do when you are sick? You are laid up in bed, so you read. And what are you going to read? What you are most curious about.

77

? Q: Wait a minute, surely school is a good thing?
A: Education is a good thing. School can be restrictive.

School can be very useful for teaching a child to read, write, learn arithmetic and pursue some specialised academic subjects, but it does not seem to promote the type of free thinkers that have historically moved society forward.

D.W. Griffith, who pioneered film directing, did not have a formal education.

Philosopher Herbert Spencer spent just three years at school and another philosopher, Benedict de Spinoza, spent a few years at school and then was expelled.

Francis Bacon, who gave us the fundamentals of scientific thought, went to school for three years, revolted against Aristotelian philosophy and left in a huff.

Benjamin Franklin spent less than two years at school.

Abraham Lincoln is revered as one of the United States' greatest presidents, who emancipated the slaves and succinctly defined democracy as 'government of the people, by the people, for the people'. His formal schooling totalled less than one year.

❓ Q: But if they don't go to school, who educates them?
■ A: They educate themselves.

Edison got his first job when he was 12 years old selling newspapers on a train that went from where he lived in Port Huron to Detroit. When the train got to Detroit he would hurry to the free public library and read before he had to catch the return train. His aim was to read every single book in the library.

All Lincoln learned at school was how to read, write and 'cipher to the rule of three', he said. There were few books or even paper on the frontier where he grew up. Lincoln used to do his arithmetic on a board. When the board was full, he would shave it clean with a drawknife and start again. He would walk long distances to borrow a book, reading it at home at the end of the day by the light of the fire.

After Franklin's formal education ended at the age of ten, he read voraciously and taught himself navigation, logic, science and several languages.

Charles Dickens was taught to read by his mother, Elizabeth. He left school at age 12 to work in a factory, though he returned for a while and left again when he was 15. What he thought of school is indicated by a quote he later made, that his headmaster was 'by far the most ignorant man' he ever had the pleasure to know.

Nikola Tesla went to the University of Prague, but did not get a degree.

Andrew Carnegie, the railroad millionaire and philanthropist, the richest man in the world of his time, did not go to school until he was seven years old. His parents told him that he did not have to go until he wanted to. They were quite relieved when he finally told them he wanted to. Carnegie left school aged 12 to work in a cotton factory, working twelve hours a day and earning $1.20 a week (by then his family had emigrated from Scotland to the US). Later he got a job as a telegraph operator. His experiences of the real world created an insatiable curiosity in him. He would borrow books from the library and read them every night.

Q: But that is in the past; surely it's different today?
A: Different, but the same.

Today, there are legal and social and pressures to stay in school, but those committed to their vocations seem to drop out and get on with it.

- ◇ Richard Branson left school when he was 17 years old.
- ◇ Bill Gates, co-founder of Microsoft, went to Harvard (planning to become a lawyer) but dropped out. He and Paul Allen (the other co-founder) started their first company while still at school, using computers to analyse traffic data for local districts to get government funding.
- ◇ Steve Jobs, founder of Apple and Pixar Animation studios, went to college but dropped out.
- ◇ Neither film directors Steven Spielberg nor Peter Jackson, or film executive Jeffrey Katzenberg (Disney, DreamWorks) have a degree.
- ◇ Billionaire Ted Turner, founder of CNN, started working for his father while still at elementary school. Turner went to college, but he did not drop out like the others. He went one better than that — he was expelled.

Q: So what's the alternative for geniuses?
A: Many of them are home-schooled.

There is a young girl in the US who is a very successful painter; she sells her paintings for about $50,000 each. By her own choice, she donates a percentage of her earnings to charity.

I saw the story on TV and it was one of those good-news stories that appear far too seldom in the media. In fact, to my mind it seemed too good to be true.

Then it was revealed on the news item that she was home-schooled. Now it made perfect sense.

? Q: So do geniuses do it alone?
A: They often have an adult who takes an interest in them.

Sometimes the adult gives them knowledge, sometimes just interest or appreciation.

Charles Dickens was told many stories of ghosts and ferocious murders by Mary Weller, his nursemaid.

Robert Louis Stevenson did not go to school much in his early years because he was ill a lot. Instead, he was read stories by his nanny, Alison Cunningham.

George Patton, the famous Second World War general who never lost a battle, was taught by his grandfather who would re-enact entire battles with him using toy soldiers.

Lincoln's stepmother had a good sense of humour. She liked to joke about how tall he was growing when he was a boy. She would tell him, 'Abe, I don't care if your feet are dirty. I can scrub the floor. But you'd better wash your head or you'll be rubbing dirt on my clean whitewashed ceiling.'

One day Lincoln saw some little boys playing in a muddy pool. He carried them to the house and held them upside down so that they walked their muddy feet across the ceiling.

When his stepmother saw the footprints, she laughed so hard she could not stand up.

? Q: How soon do geniuses start?
A: As soon as possible.

Many geniuses simply start early in their chosen profession. Perhaps it's not so much how clever they are, but that they actually get started.

The legendary performer Sammy Davis Jr. started his career aged three. He never really went to school, but while he was serving in the army, and influenced by a sergeant, he developed a voracious appetite for reading.

Charlie Chaplin entered the theatre aged nine.

Gunther Gebel-Williams was the greatest circus act of the twentieth century. His mother was in the circus and he left school at 12 to travel with her. When she decided to leave the circus, Williams stayed and the circus owners took him on as a son. Then his education in the whole circus world truly began. Williams explained his success by saying, 'Not so many people like to take the time to learn something very well — and almost nobody wants to take the time to learn everything about anything.' He trained tigers, giraffes, elephants and goats. He even trained his wife (to be a circus performer) when he saw her sitting in the audience at one of his shows.

He famously performed one routine called 'Propulsion by Pachyderm Power', where one elephant would stamp on a see-saw that would throw Williams up into the air. He would then somersault and land triumphantly on the back of another elephant. Another routine involved two horses, two tigers and two elephants all on stage at the same time; Williams would position the tigers, horses and elephants on top of each other and then straddle them all with his hands raised in the air in victory. Don't try that at home!

? Q: Are geniuses perfect?
A: A person who can't make a mistake can't make anything.

While the school system attempts to turn out perfect people (trying to get 100% in their exams), instilling in them a fear of making mistakes, geniuses are more than happy to make mistakes.

There once was a little boy who was born in a ladies' toilet at a dance. He grew up a lonely child because there was a six-year age gap between himself and his brother and his parents were distant. The boy had a lisp and a stutter. And he did poorly at school. His school reports described him as, 'very bad … a constant trouble to everybody'. The boy liked to play with toy soldiers and so his father decided that the military was a good career for someone of limited intelligence. The boy was sent to take the examination for the Royal Military Academy at Sandhurst. He failed. He tried again. He failed again. Clearly, this boy was destined for a life of failure, so it is doubtful if you have ever heard his name. I will tell it to you anyway.

It was Winston Churchill. He became a great orator and author, won the Nobel Prize in Literature in 1953 and led Britain out of the hell of the Second World War.

❓ Q: How do you draw the genius out of someone?
■ A: Challenge them.

> *A real warrior takes everything as a challenge.*
> — *Carlos Castaneda*

Challenge actually comes from the Latin word *calumnia*, from which we derive the word calumny, meaning 'slander'. In other words, to challenge was to face something that was threatening your honour.

Alexander Graham Bell was at first taught at home with his brothers by his mother, who was deaf. They communicated to her in sign language. At the age of 11, he was sent to Royal Edinburgh High School and hated it. Bell was often absent and his grades were poor. His only interests were maths and science, virtually ignoring the other subjects. After leaving school at the age of 15, he stayed with his grandfather in London, who took an interest in him. The older man listened to him, had serious discussions with him and challenged him. Out of this, a love of learning was born in the young man.

Bell's father encouraged an interest he had developed in speech and took him to see a 'mechanical man' that simulated human speech, which had been built by a German inventor. Afterwards, Bell got hold of the book the inventor had written on the subject and laboriously translated it into English. Spurred on by their father, who offered a 'big prize', Bell and his brother succeeded in creating a crude apparatus, powered by a bellows, that could articulate the word 'mama'.

Bell then experimented with the family dog until it could produce a sound that — with a little imagination from the listener — could be heard as, 'How are you grandma?' It was the world's first talking dog.

Q: Can people challenge themselves?
A: That's called demand.

Geniuses do not wait for things to happen. They go out and create them and they demand of themselves and others the highest standards. They set targets and drive themselves to meet them.

Q: Are you saying that by challenging someone, they can become a genius?
A: Theoretically, that's true.

Try it.

Chapter 3
Society

The first point at which the child usually interacts with society is during their education. Do you remember that first day when you were taken out of the warm intimacy of the family home and thrust into the strange new environment called school?

Education

What is the purpose of an education system?

A **To create a well-rounded individual.**

In other words, someone with the corners (individuality) knocked off them, who will respect society, obey the law, do what they're told, hold down a steady job, pay their taxes and be a quiet cog in a giant machine.

❓ Q: What would happen to a society if everybody was like that?
A: It would shrink into insignificance.

At one time, the mighty Roman Empire ruled the known world. Why did it fall? Everybody knows that it was because the barbarians invaded it. But Rome was a superpower and the invaders were just a bunch of hooligans.

The truth was that under the thumb of the suffocating bureaucracy that Rome had become, the citizens did not have sufficient spirit left to even issue the invaders with a parking ticket. The barbarians were wild, but at least they could think for themselves.

❓ Q: What is education supposed to be?
A: A way of making the individual more powerful.

Life is either a daring adventure or nothing.
— *Helen Keller*

Education comes from the Latin *e* meaning 'out' and *ducere*, 'to lead or draw', so education is actually the process of leading or drawing out the individual. In our modern education system all the traffic is going the other way. The individual is being overwhelmed by a continual assault of facts. These are then supposed to be regurgitated in examinations. This is not education. This is an academic system. And the system is suppressing the individual. True education is the joy of discovery and if it ain't that, it ain't education.

❓ Q: What is the purpose of education?
A: To help people think for themselves.

❓ Q: What is the antithesis of education?
A: Telling people what to think or telling them to stop thinking.

In 496 AD the Roman Catholic Church decreed that certain books were to be banned. A new list was issued in 1559 entitled *Index Librorum Prohibitorum* (Index of Forbidden Books). The penalty for reading one of them was excommunication. It was not until 1966 that the index was finally discontinued and excommunication lifted.

In 1875, the director of the US Patent Office tendered his resignation and suggested that the department be closed on the grounds that there was nothing left to invent.

In Germany during the 1930s, Nazi party members conducted book-burning orgies for books that they did not agree with.

Q: Do people also close their own minds?
A: Unfortunately, yes.

In 1937, Sylvan N. Goldman of Oklahoma City had the brilliant idea of inventing supermarket trolleys (before that people lugged heavy baskets around). He found, however, that nobody would use them because they did not want other people to think they were weak. So Goldman had to go out and hire professional 'trolley pushers' pretending to be shoppers to get people to start using the carts.

Benjamin Franklin said, 'The doors of wisdom are never shut.' Ideally they are flung open as wide as barn doors.

Q: How did education come about?
A: It started with grandparents.

At first, education was right on the spot: fathers of the tribe would go out hunting; mothers would go out gathering berries; those left behind were either too young or too old to go. The too old (grandparents) would pass on necessary skills to the too young (children). So, grandparents really were the first teachers.

Q: What is the best education?
A: Self-education.

Some things you need to figure out for yourself. The main problem with any education system that has ever been invented is that it is trying to mass-produce something that cannot be mass-produced — an individual.

Q: What is the most important thing in education?
A: Curiosity.

The main rule of the schoolmaster is not to impart knowledge,
but to build an appetite for it and the means of gaining it.
— Thomas Arnold (1795–1842) Headmaster of Rugby School

Though generally overlooked, curiosity accounts for probably 50% of all learning.

Have you ever noticed the eager glow,
On the face of the child that wants to know?

Q: What are the foundations of learning?
A: What used to be called reading, writing and 'rithmetic.

Don't you love it that educators had sufficient sense of humour to deliberately misspell one of their foundations of learning?

Q: Why are these so important?
A: They mark the starting point of the two great branches of knowledge.

All knowledge basically breaks down into *quantity* and *quality*.

Quantity is defined by mathematics, which comes from the Greek word for measuring. Maths is simply the science of: *How much? How long? How many?*

How many is numbers. Arithmetic is the part of maths that deals with numbers. It comes from the Greek *arithmos* meaning 'numbers' and *tehkne* or 'art'; the art of controlling numbers. Very rich businesspeople actually use only basic arithmetic. Most people don't use it at all other than to count their loose change.

We use language to define quality. Quality asks *of what kind?* The girl is wearing a hat. What kind of hat is it? It is a red hat. Red is the quality that sets it apart from other hats. 'I have one red hat', shows both the quality and the quantity of the hat.

Q: What is grammar?
A: The person married to grandpa.

Seriously, grammar refers to the rules of how language is used, rules that have evolved out of common usage. It comes from the Greek *gramma* meaning 'letters'. Not understanding grammar is like playing tennis without fully knowing the rules.

Q: What is the key to learning?
A: Understanding words.

It has been found that the primary failure to understanding is failing to comprehend the meaning of a word, or thinking that you understand a word but have the wrong definition for it.

Q: What is the solution to this?
A: Looking up the word in a dictionary.

The use of dictionaries and the understanding of words is the key to all knowledge. Each word has an exact definition, like having a fence around it. When a person strays into the wrong definition, their thinking becomes muddled. When words have been looked up in the dictionary, a person's thinking becomes crystal clear and they are articulate in speech and writing.

When New Zealand-born Eric Partridge was eight years old, his father had an argument with a neighbour about whether an insect that had buzzed past them was called a bumblebee or a humble bee. Partridge's father insisted it was humble bee. Partridge consulted his dictionary and was disappointed to discover that only the bumblebee was listed. It seemed that his father was wrong.

Years later, Partridge became a famous lexicographer (writer of dictionaries) who became known as The Word Man. One day while doing his research he came across *humble bee*. He found that it had first been written down in about 1450, while *bumblebee* dated back to only 1530. So his father had been right after all.

Another word for bumblebee is dumbledore, the name J.K. Rowling gave to the headmaster of Hogwarts in her *Harry Potter* series.

Q: Can a little word really be so important?
A: Language is a complex web, full of subtle traps.

One of the disasters in the space programme — with loss of life — followed confusion among engineers between yards and metres.

The English language consists of over 500,000 words, many of which have been developing for thousands of years. A person does not need to know all these words, since many of them are specialised, but they must understand that mastering words is the key to success in modern society (it's no longer hunting mammoths, as it was in the past).

Q: When studying a subject, how do you unlock it?
A: Here are the keys:

First, understand the scope of the subject by looking the subject itself up in a dictionary. This will give you the exact definition and limit of what the subject covers. You also need to discover:

◇ its purpose;

◇ its importance;

◇ how it fits in with other subjects;

◇ what use it is to you personally.

You should also clearly understand the key words of the subject and know the key rules of the subject.

Q: What are the main branches of knowledge and how do they fit together?
A: Usually they are considered to be the following:

◇ Mathematics measures things — *how much?*;

◇ Language uses written or spoken symbols to describe quality — *what?*;

◇ Science explains how the physical world works — *how?*;

◇ History accounts for what has happened in the past — *when?*;

◇ Geography explains location — *where?*;

◇ Humanities look at people and their interaction — *who?*;

◇ The arts are forms of creativity — *in which ways?*;

◇ Religion or spirituality is about origin and purpose — *why?*;

◇ Curiosity — *if.*

Curiosity isn't usually found anywhere as a subject; however, it is the driving force for all knowledge.

Q: What exactly is language?
A: It is the main method used to communicate ideas.

Langauge developed as a spoken sound code to describe the physical world. The word 'tree' originally meant 'a tall thing dressed in leaves'. A word represents an idea. The idea represents a real object. Or it represents a concept, such as happiness.

Q: What does spoken language consist of?
A: It's a sandwich.

Most languages are a sandwich of consonants and vowels.

A consonant is a spoken sound that is obstructed by some part of the mouth before it is emitted, such as lips, tongue, teeth. For example p, b, f. Consonants are the bread.

A vowel passes right through without being obstructed by anything. The vowel (from the Latin *vocal*) sounds in English are a, e, i, o, u. They are the peanut butter in the sandwich.

❓ Q: What is a sentence?
■ A: A complete thought.

The cat sat on the mat is a complete thought. *The cat* or *on the mat* are not sentences because on their own they don't make sense. You are left hanging, waiting for the full thought.

❓ Q: What is a paragraph?
■ A: A collection of sentences on the same subject.

> *The others whispered together.*
>
> (new subject therefore new paragraph)
>
> *At length, Madame Aloise, who was no less jealous because she so admired her own daughter, addressed the dancing girl.*
> — From *The Hunchback of Notre Dame* by Victor Hugo.

A paragraph can be as short or as long as you want, as long as it sticks to one subject.

❓ Q: What are the most common parts of grammar?
■ A: As follows.

A *noun* is something that exists.	A *ball*
A *verb* tells you the action that takes place.	A ball *rolls*
An *adjective* is a describing word.	A *red* ball rolls
A *conjunction* joins a groups of words.	The ball rolls *and* rolls
A *preposition* shows position or relationships.	The ball rolls and rolls *until* it stops

❓ Q: Are there different types of verbs?
■ A: Yes, because verbs control time.

In verbs, time is called tense (from the Latin *tendere*, or 'stretch'). The main tenses are:

◇ present   the ball *rolls*

◇ past   the ball *rolled*

◇ future   the ball *will roll*

◇ possibility   the ball *could roll*

Q: What is punctuation?

A: Symbols that show the breaths you would take if you were speaking.

The word punctuation comes from the Latin *pungere* meaning 'to prick'. The main symbols are:

- full stop or period long pause, take a breath (also the end of the sentence)

, comma short pause, quick breath

? question mark used when asking a question

! exclamation mark a stronger form of expression

: colon take a big breath, going to make a big statement

; semicolon take a smaller breath than colon, going to make a smaller statement

" quotation marks repeating exactly what someone has said

- hyphen pause because the next bit is joined

However the problem with the theory of punctuation is that some men reckon women can talk for hours without breathing!

❓ Q: What the heck is prose?
■ A: Normal spoken or written language.

Prose comes from the Latin *prorsus* meaning 'direct'. It is arranged into sentences, but it's no more ordered than that. This book has been written in prose.

❓ Q: What the heck is poetry?
■ A: It's measured out and often rhymes.

> I am the fish that swims,
> In ocean dark and deep,
> Through the resting wreck,
> That rusts in restless sleep.

Poetry comes from the Greek *poesis* which means 'to make'.

❓ Q: What the heck is a metaphor?
■ A: *Sea of troubles* is one.

That's from Hamlet's famous 'To be or not to be' speech. A metaphor is when you take something real and use it to express an abstract quality (one that does not physically exist). The word *sea* implies the savagery of nature, a powerful enemy, storms and shipwrecks, lending those real images and even emotions to the abstract quality of *troubles*. The word 'metaphor' comes from the Greek *meta* or 'change' and *pherein*, 'carry': in other words, to carry across or transfer.

❓ Q: What is rhetoric?
■ A: It is great writing or speaking.

Rhetoric is when all the tools of language are used to express ideas with clarity and emotion.

> *As the war lengthens and intensifies and the extending lists appear, it seems as if one watched at night a well-loved city whose lights, which burn so true, are extinguished in the distance in the darkness one by one.* — Winston Churchill, on the death of a friend and fellow officer in the Second World War

The word 'rhetoric' comes from the Greek *rhetor* meaning 'orator'. Churchill was a great orator.

? Q: Just run it by me again, what exactly is maths?
A: A method of predicting, controlling and communicating with the physical world.

If you try to talk to a stone, it does not talk back. It is in inanimate object, lacking life. The essential method you use to communicate with it and to control it is maths. Mentally, you measure how far to reach to pick up the stone, the pressure your fingers need to exert to grip it and how hard you have to throw it to get it to land in the river.

Building rockets is more complex, but basically the same.

? Q: Why is maths so difficult to understand?
A: It's all Greek to me.

No, seriously it is all Greek. And Arabic. They pioneered the subject of maths, so we use their terminology. To fully understand the terms, you have to use a dictionary to find the original meanings of those words.

? Q: Why can maths be so boring sometimes?
A: Because maths translates reality into symbols.

The real world is massive and often majestic.

Maths takes three-dimensional reality and reduces it down to symbols. A symbol is a sign of the reality, not the reality itself. After a while, too many symbols on their own can become boring.

If you tried to explain how a car engine works to a small child — without letting them look at an engine or draw it or even use objects to represent the parts of it — after a while they would get bored and grumpy. They would start to revolt. The same can happen with maths. All symbols without reality gets boring. Even exasperating.

The antidote to this is to replace the lost reality through sketching, using objects to represent it or sometimes even viewing the reality itself or photographs of it.

❓ Q: What is geometry?
■ A: Space maths.

Geometry is the maths of measuring space. Ancient humans thought of space as land area, so we have *geo* meaning 'earth' and *metre*, 'measure', literally measuring the earth. Spaces are determined by points, straight lines, angles and so on.

❓ Q: What is algebra?
■ A: Detective maths.

Algebra is the maths of finding an absent quantity, just like the detective following the clues (the known facts) towards the biggest unknown: discovering the murderer.

In algebra, known amounts are used to discover unknown amounts. Until discovered, letters such as *x* or *y* are used to represent the unknown quantities. The word 'algebra' comes from the Arabic *al-jabr* which literally means 'bone setting'. Possibly this referred to *setting right with what you have* or reconstructing the bones of a skeleton (trying to work out where the bones go).

❓ Q: What is calculus?
■ A: Moving maths.

Calculus is the maths of moving quantities. When you count your loose change, the coins sit still to be counted. That is arithmetic. When you calculate the flight of a plane, not only is it travelling, but gravity is trying to pull it down and wind is trying to blow it off course. That is calculus.

In Latin, *calculus* is a small pebble that was used on abacuses. Calculus got man to the moon. After that, he took the bus home.

❓ Q: What is science?
■ A: How the physical universe works.

Science is understanding the natural laws of the universe and harnessing them.

When the Romans attacked the town of Syracuse in ancient Greece, they were astonished to find huge boulders were being tossed at them by giant catapults, and mechanical cranes reached out into the harbour and turned over their ships. Massive lenses set fire to their ships by focusing the rays of the sun on them. To the Romans it must have been like being in a science-fiction movie.

But these were all inventions of the great scientist Archimedes.

Q: What is physics?
A: The science of how forces operate.

In 1654 Otto von Guericke conducted an experiment before the Holy Roman Emperor. He greased the edges of two copper hemispheres and, using a special pump, sucked the air out of them before fastening them together. He attached a horse to each sphere and whipped them to pull them apart. But the seal did not break. He kept adding horses and only when he had eight horses pulling on each side did the seal actually break. He had demonstrated the power of the vacuum.

Q: What is chemistry?
A: The science of how matter changes.

Matter is the solid particles of the universe. They do not stay the same but change form. For example, water is made up of hydrogen and oxygen combining. When you boil water, you separate them.

Q: What are Newton's Three Laws of Motion?
A: Inertia, motion and reaction.

Inertia (from Greek *in* meaning 'not' and *ars* or 'art'. Art is movement and creativity. It takes energy to create and it moves people, at least emotionally. Therefore inertia is the opposite — no movement): an object at rest will tend to stay at rest. An object in motion will tend to stay in motion.

So a ball lying on a flat surface will not move until something causes it to move. A rolling ball will not stop rolling until something stops it, such as an obstruction or gravity.

Motion: if you apply force to something, it will move in the direction and to the degree of that force. If you kick the ball towards the goal it will tend to move towards the goal (unless you are taking it for the English football team in a penalty shoot-out).

Reaction: an action creates an opposite equal reaction. If you drop a ball, it will bounce.

❓ Q: What is an atom?
■ A: The smallest particle of matter.

A piece of paper is about one million atoms thick. An atom has a nucleus in the centre with a proton and electron whizzing around it. An atom is really a miniature version of the solar system with the nucleus as the Sun and the others as the planets.

❓ Q: Who was the first person to split the atom?
■ A: Ernest Rutherford.

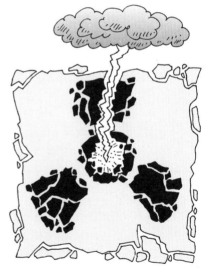

Q: Who put it back together again?
A: Ha ha. Very funny.

Q: If Rutherford was a physicist, why did he win the Nobel Prize in Chemistry?
A: Bureaucracy.

No one was more amused by this than Rutherford himself. He had once succeeded in changing nitrogen into oxygen by bombarding nitrogen gas with particles. But he said that going from a physicist to a chemist was his greatest transformation.

Q: What is the difference between chemistry and physics?
A: In chemistry things change, in physics they stay the same.

If you soak the dishes in water before washing up, the chemical action of the water and the washing-up liquid partially cleans the dishes. This is chemistry. When you use 'elbow grease' to clean them, that is physics.

Q: What is biology?
A: Biology is the science of living things.

This is plants and animals. Biology comes from the Greek *bio* for 'life' and *logos* for 'knowledge'.

Q: What is history?
A: Depends who you ask.

Some say history is a lot of bunk, some say it is just the stories of the victors. But the man known as the father of history, the Greek Herodotus (484–425 BC), wisely said, 'Those who are ignorant of history are forced to relive it.'

Q: How did education become an academic system?
A: By Plato starting his Academy.

In ancient Greece, children did not actually go to school as such. A slave would take them to different teachers who specialised in different subjects. Then in about 387 BC Plato founded perhaps the first school (of philosophy) called the Academy and thus academic education was born.

Students gathered there to listen to him speak and it has remained the same ever since. One person yapping and the rest listening.

❓ Q: How did governments come to control education?
A: Because they realised it gave them more influence over the people.

After the fall of Rome and the coming of the Dark Ages, the Christian Church was the only stability most people had in their lives. They relied on it and so it took out a monopoly on knowledge. As detailed in the introduction, the invention of the printing press led to democracy.

In Europe during the 1700s, new nations arose that wanted to turn a person's primary allegiance away from God, to patriotism for their country. After the French Revolution, the French government took over all the schools in the country.

In Prussia they developed a national school system that, in 1871, enabled the King of Prussia to become the first emperor of a united Germany.

When other countries saw the key part that education had in this, they also began to nationalise education.

❓ Q: But America is the land of the free. How did it happen there?
A: Similar story.

In 1636 the Massachusetts Bay Colony founded Harvard College, which later became Harvard University. That year the colony passed a law that every town with at least 50 families had to start an elementary school. Though there was some public funding, the schools were basically independent.

Then, after the Civil War, a strategy was developed to unify America. A national school system was instituted and textbooks were produced, which as well as giving information about reading and spelling, started to indoctrinate Americans into *what they were supposed to be*, which was mainly white, Protestant, honest and hard-working.

Other races such as the Spanish and the Native American Indians were denigrated as inferior.

Today, with a few exceptions, all education in America is state-funded and controlled.

Q: When did school attendance first become compulsory?
A: 1494.

The first compulsory education in Britain was in 1494 when a Scottish act compelled all barons and freeholders to send their sons to school. The 1880 Education Act made school compulsory between the ages of five and ten. The school leaving age has been regularly raised over the years and in most countries it is now set at 16. Some cynics claim that raising it is just an attempt to massage the unemployment figures.

Q: When should a person be allowed to leave school?
A: When it's right for them.

There are some children who probably don't ever need to go to school. Many don't, being home-schooled. Many very successful people in the past left school at 13 and went straight into a job or an apprenticeship.

A person currently spends about 12 years at school, about 15 years if tertiary study is included in that. Some are spending about a quarter of their lives in school, preparing themselves for a life they are waiting to start. Sometimes it is better just to start.

A teacher once sat next to a little girl on a bus and said to her, 'I am a grown-up, but I am still at school. What do you think I must be?'

The little girl replied, 'I think you must be very stupid.'

Q: Does learning stop after you leave school?
A: No, it should increase.

The person who keeps learning is the one who will succeed.

Identity

Between childhood and adulthood are the teenage years, which can be very exciting, but also sometimes a gauntlet, during which, sooner or later they will achieve that great collision with society known as a *job*.

What is a teenager?

An alien life form.

Sign on wall: No spitting, excessive noise or skateboarding.

Teenager: Why don't they just say *No Teenagers*?

Q: When were teenagers invented?
A: It's not a joke. Teenagers are a manufactured species.

Technically, a teenager is anyone between the ages of 13 and 19, but the new leisure class of being a 'teenager' only came into being in the years following the Second World War, when labour-saving devices made life easier. Before that, young people were too busy helping the family put food on the table to be 'teenagers'.

Q: What is puberty?
A: The point when a child starts to physically change into an adult.

Technically, puberty is the time, between the ages of 12 and 14, when a human is physiologically able to produce a child, marked by the arrival of pubic hair and often accompanied by growth spurts.

In boys, the voice breaks and the testes start to produce sperm.

In girls, menstruation starts for the first time and eggs are produced.

? Q: What is juvenile delinquency?
A: Rebellion instead of revelry.

Children misbehave because they are not being challenged.

Part of being challenged is being allowed to contribute. If they are not allowed to contribute they rebel. The word 'rebel' comes from Latin *re* meaning 'again' and *bellum*, 'war; to fight against'. The word 'revel', one of the meanings of which is 'to take keen delight in', also comes from the same root. In other words, if you are not allowed to revel (participate) in something, you will rebel.

Child labour laws, which were formed long ago to stop young children being forced to sweep chimneys, now actually stop the young from working, creating a culture of enforced indolence.

We should relax the laws to allow the young to work.

We should take the graffiti artists and pay them to paint something constructive.

We should take teenage rebellion and turn it into a revolution of revelry.

Q: What are gangs?
A: A country within a country.

People join gangs to gain a sense of belonging.

They don't feel part of the group of their family or school or whatever, so they join a group they feel they can be part of.

One Christmas, purely for pleasure, I read a book about the gangs of the world — the Mafia (Sicily and the US), Camorra (Naples), Yakuza (Japan) and others. I was surprised to find that each gang had been formed by the government of that country. Not intentionally, but in some way the government had excluded people from being normal citizens, and so in response the dispossessed had formed their own country within a country.

Q: Why do people take drugs?
A: As a substitute for happiness.

Drugs dull pain, whether physical or spiritual. They numb a part of the person. As the person becomes more addicted to them, the drugs slowly and surely erase the person.

? Q: When should a rite of passage into adulthood occur?
■ A: As soon as possible.

In the Jewish religion, the rite of passage at about the age of 13 is called the bar mitzvah. It is when a child becomes fully responsible for their own actions (which is basically the definition of adulthood).

Around the world there are many unusual rites of passage such as the one on the South Pacific island of Vanuatu where, for thousands of years, the locals have been tying vines around their ankles and jumping off a wooden tower 25 metres high. This led to the commercial sport of bungee jumping.

According to legend this was all started by a woman who was being pursued by her jealous husband. She climbed a tree and threw herself out of it. Not wanting to live without her he did the same and was killed. But she cunningly had tied vines around her ankle and lived.

One rite of passage in modern civilisation is the debutante ball (a version is the high school prom) which usually occurs at about the age of 18. A less stylish variation of this is getting drunk on your 18th birthday.

For some who are more intellectual, the rite of passage into adulthood has become a graduation ceremony at the end of college, dressing up in a cap and gown and tossing the cap high into the air.

Traditionally in Japan, boys between the ages of 12 and 16 were taken to the shrines of their patron, given new adult names and presented with their first adult clothes. A similar ceremony was performed for girls between the ages of 12 and 14.

In modern Japan, these have now been replaced by coming-of-age ceremonies which take place at the age of 20 (for both sexes).

There seems to be an unfortunate trend in modern society where rites of passage are occurring later, slowing down the maturing of the child into an independent adult.

❓ Q: What is work?
A: The reason why we get up in the mornings.

Most people would be lost without a job to go to, and many suffer loss of morale and confidence when unemployed.

We all need some form of work to get the money to survive. But is it satisfying or is it drudgery? Here is a scale of types of work:

VOCATION

PROFESSION

CAREER

JOB

STUDENT

UNEMPLOYED

CRIMINAL

Where are you on the scale? Are you following your true calling in life? If not, what is the next step up the scale?

Chapter 4
Humanity

Humanity consists of a rich variety of creeds, colours and races, all struggling to get on with each other at times.

What is the biggest problem in the human race?

A **When one of the races tries to *win* the race.**

If only we could all get on. As the Italians say, 'The whole world is one family.'

Q: What is culture?
A: The sum of all the traditions and customs of a group of people.

Customs generally develop over time.

An important part of culture is manners. These form set procedures that assist people to get along with each other.

The handshake, for example, came about from when two knights would meet. They would hold out their right hand (their sword hand) to show that it was empty and therefore they were a friend.

? Q: How did cultures spread?
A: Originally by traders such as Marco Polo.

In 1271 at the age of 17, Marco Polo travelled to China from Italy with his father and uncle. They crossed mountains and deserts (the Taklamakan Desert was known by the locals as the Land of Irrevocable Death) and after three-and-a-half years they finally arrived in China.

For the next 17 years, Marco Polo travelled as an ambassador of Kublai Khan. When he, his father and uncle finally arrived home, they were not recognised. They had long been believed to be dead and their possessions divided up.

Marco Polo wrote a book about his travels, describing fabulous palaces, crocodiles and giraffes (unseen in the West at that time), men with tails (monkeys) and unicorns (rhinoceroses). The book was generally believed to be a work of fiction and became a best-seller.

? Q: What is a country?
A: A collection of people with the same prejudices.

Countries were originally formed by natural barriers such as seas, rivers and mountains, or by artificial ones such as war, which lead to people forming a mutually protective grouping.

? Q: Why are people so patriotic?
Answer 1: Because they have a genuine love of their homeland.

They revel in the customs, humour, arts and sport of the culture they were brought up in and are proud to be identified with it.

? Q: Why are people so patriotic?
■ Answer 2: Patriotism maintains the status quo.

The status quo (Latin for 'how things stand') has the power and the money. The mass media tends to work for the status quo because it has the money and the owners of the media want some of its money. Patriotism is also actively maintained through the mass media by sport ('Support our team at the World Cup') and trade ('Buy British').

This keeps everyone warmed up for the fervent rallying call of when old men in government seek to send young men overseas to 'die for their country'.

The basis of war is country first; before God, family and the individual.

? Q: What is the haka?
■ A: It is a war dance.

War dances were traditionally used by Maori to show respect, protest, defiance, triumph, or to issue a challenge. It is performed by the All Black rugby team of New Zealand before playing to let their opponents know they are going to be in for one hell of a match.

? Q: What do the words of the haka mean in English?

A: This is a translation of the traditional *Ka Mate* haka:

Ka Mate	It is Death
A ka mate! ka mate!	It is death! It is death!
Ka ora! Ka ora!	It is life! It is life!
Ka mate! Ka mate!	It is death! It is death!
Ka ora! Ka ora!	It is life! It is life!
Tenei te tangata puhuru huru	Look! There stands the hairy man
Nana nei i tiki mai whakawhiti te ra!	Who will cause the sun to shine!
A hupane! A kaupane!	One step upwards, another step upwards!
A hupane! A kaupane!	One step upwards, another step upwards!
Whiti te ra!	The sun shines!

Q: What is it about?
A: A Maori chief who escapes death.

In about 1820 the chief Te Rauparaha was being pursued by his enemies and so hid in the kumara (a sweet potato) pit of a friendly chief, Te Wharerangi. As Te Rauparaha's enemies approached, they chanted incantations to try and prevent him escaping the area.

Sitting alone in the dark pit, Te Rauparaha could feel the incantations starting to take effect on him. Te Wharerangi's wife, Te Rangikoaea, then stood astride the entrance to the kumara pit, neutralising the incantations of the pursuers.

Even so, as he heard the tramp of his enemies' feet above, Te Rauparaha was beset by fear and muttered to himself, 'It is death!' Then, when he thought the enemy were not far off, he muttered, 'It is life!' But when they did not depart, he muttered again, 'It is death!' Later, as his pursuers finally left he said, 'It is life!'

Cautiously Te Rauparaha climbed out of the pit, 'One step upwards, another step upwards!' until at last he was outside and shouted exultantly, 'The sun shines!'

? Q: How did government come about?
A: From the old village-chief system.

In order for a large group of people to combine their efforts, they usually need a leader. So in the past they elected one and he was given a share of their harvest.

In time everyone forgot that the leader was there to serve, and so instead of making voluntary contributions it became compulsory and that became tax. Now they had a government.

? Q: How do laws come about?
A: Out of the customs of the people.

Laws develop from the customs of the people. If you murdered someone, for example, it was seen to be bad for their health. And so murder became illegal.

Laws that do not follow the customs of the people are virtually unenforceable, such as when Prohibition made alcohol illegal in the US at the beginning of the twentieth century.

Whether drinking alcohol is good for people or not, it was an established custom. The people carried on drinking anyway and the direct result of this law was to make the Mafia powerful — they were the only ones who could supply alcohol because it was illegal and so were they.

? Q: How did the British royal family come to power?
A: This noble institution is the result of a long line of murderers, thieves and sadists.

There was Henry VIII, who invented divorce and nationalised the church and ripped off its wealth.

There was Richard III, who murdered two young boys who were contenders for the throne.

And people complain about Prince Harry! He's an angel by comparison.

The founder of the current dynasty, William the Conqueror, was a sensitive new-age guy who tried to force the town of Exeter to give up a siege by standing before its walls and, in view of the defenders, blinding a hostage.

By the time he died, William had become so overweight that they could not get his body into his stone tomb. Also his body had actually burst and emitted a foul smell. Few of his nobles bothered to attend to the pong or the funeral. Instead they rushed off to their own estates to prepare for the power struggle that would come.

The King is dead.

Long live the stink!

? Q: What was the worst disaster that ever befell the royal family?
A: The milk supply got cut off.

What happened was that Charles I (who was the King) was accused of treason against the King. It's a bit like being accused of murdering yourself.

There was a trial and Charles was found guilty. As King he probably could have pardoned himself, but they would not let him and he ended up getting his head chopped off.

Then Oliver Cromwell and the Puritans came to power, but they were so miserable that everyone wanted the King back. They tried to stick Charles' head back on his body, but it didn't fit, so they got his son Charles II to be King instead.

However, in the confusion they forgot one very important thing. They forgot to restore the old custom that the infant heir to the throne, as Prince of Wales, was always suckled on the bosom of a Welsh wet nurse.

The absence of that healthy Welsh milk in the succeeding generations explains a lot.

? Q: How did communism come about?
A: Because of the fascists.

Communism was started by the German Secret Service.

Russia was fighting against Germany in the First World War and the Germans wanted to take them out of the war. Lenin was in exile in Europe and so the Germans shipped him back to Russia on a special train to start the Russian Revolution.

? Q: What is war?
A: The bane of humanity.

When the American general W.T. Sherman addressed the Michigan Military Academy in 1879 he said, 'I am tired and sick of war. Its glory is all moonshine. It is only those who have neither fired a shot, nor heard the shrieks and groans of the wounded, who cry aloud for blood, more vengeance, more desolation. War is hell.'

? Q: What is the history of warfare?
A: People killing each other from further and further away.

Warfare began with men fighting each other on foot. In those days, you got to meet your enemy face to face, exchange names and possibly even invite him around for dinner.

Then they started getting further apart with the inventions of javelins, arrows and machines. In the twentieth century killing became mechanised and mass-produced.

Today it has reached the point where you do not even have to be in the same country to lob missiles at each other. As it says on the joke army recruiting T-shirt: 'Join the army, travel the world, meet fascinating people ... and kill them.'

Charming!

? Q: Is a war waged for honour and glory?
A: No. For resources and money.

War is fought for land. You always have to ask what rich resources the land produces.

? Q: What do you need to convince people to fight a war?
A: A just cause.

A just cause is a noble-sounding idea that people will buy into. Here is a short table of some wars, with their just causes and the real reasons why they were fought:

War	Just Cause	Real Reason
Trojan War (c. 1184 BC)	Helen was abducted	Trade routes to Constantinople
Boxer Rebellion, China (1900)	Protect foreign nationals	Drugs
Boer War (1899–1902)	Protect British nationals	Gold under the Transvaal
Afghanistan (2001–)	Democracy	Drugs (?)
Iraq (2003–)	Weapons of Mass Destruction	Oil

? Q: But surely, wars are not always fought for riches?
A: One battle was fought for shoes.

It was the Battle of Gettysburg in the American Civil War.

Shoes were the goal of a brigade of barefoot rebels when they arrived at a frontier town of America's West. Another road into the town brought in a brigade of Yankees and since the two were at war with each other, they naturally started shooting at each other.

From such banal beginnings this escalated into a bloody battle with

50,000 casualties. Twenty thousand rifles were found abandoned on the battlefield afterwards with not one, but both bullets, still lodged in the breech. Forget the Wild West; these were untrained, terrified soldiers blundering to war.

Even more fearful were their own surgeons, who sawed off limbs with blunt tools and without anaesthetic, leaving a pile of severed limbs outside the surgeon's tent, as high as a man was tall.

And all for shoes.

Q: What was the result of the American Civil War?
Answer 1: The emancipation of the slaves.

Q: What was the result of the American Civil War?
Answer 2: The growth of war profiteers.

The war was very profitable for Colt's Manufacturing Company, and probably started the armaments industry (they use the euphemism *aerospace* today) which vies with entertainment as the biggest export earner in the US.

It was also around this time that the newspaper industry took off in the US. Papers doubled in size, most carrying advertisements for a host of quack medicines that promised to relieve the war veterans of their suffering. This may have been the birth of the multi billion-dollar pharmaceutical industry. Coca-Cola (which originally contained cocaine) was originally marketed as a palliative for war wounds.

Q: Do you need a scapegoat for a war?
A: Ask the expert. Ask Adolf.

Adolf Hitler once said, 'Any revolution must find a scapegoat as a lightning rod for the odium of the masses.'

He chose the Jews because they already had a history of persecution. This stemmed partly from the fact that, according to the Bible, Christians were not supposed to borrow money from their brothers. Since the Bible also taught that the Jews had killed Christ, they could not be considered brothers. In these early times, there were a range of prohibitions on Jews and many became the money-lenders since this was one of the only professions they were allowed to have. As a result, they became quite wealthy and, it seems, even more unpopular.

Today some people are trying to make the Muslims the scapegoats. Different religion, same old story.

Q: What is the real cause of war?
A: Someone stirring up a conflict to make a profit out of it.

In the nineteenth century the Rothschild Bank played all the newly independent (and very patriotic) countries in Europe off against each other — they loaned money to both sides to fund wars out of which the bank made large profits.

In 1886 gold was discovered in the Transvaal in South Africa, causing tensions between the local Boers and the colonial British. Sir Arthur Milner, Governor of the Cape Colony, pretended to intercede, but he had made a secret alliance with two gold magnates, Beit and Warner. He admitted in his private letters that, 'It would have been easy to patch things up … and to settle the differences with the Uitlanders.' Instead he precipitated the war for selfish gain. He never did get his gold and left South Africa.

Years later he returned, only to be killed by a tsetse fly.

Q: Who invented the concentration camp?
A: No it wasn't Adolf, it was the British.

During the Second Boer War (1899–1902), British Field Marshal Horatio Herbert Kitchener rounded up the Boer women and children and put them into concentration camps where thousands died of disease and starvation. The Boers responded with dumdum bullets (ammunition which had been hollowed out to explode on impact). It became so bad that neither side paid any respect to the white flag.

Q: Is there any glory in war?
A: That is what we have been led to believe.

But it doesn't make sense.

When your favourite football team loses, is that also glorious?

When a player gets injured, is that glorious?

Where is the glory in killing other people? Or getting killed yourself?

In the trenches of the First World War there was a soldier who came down with dysentery and his friends had to help him to go to the latrines. He was in such a bad way that he actually fell into the latrine, and before his mates could get him out he had drowned.

Drowned in his own excrement!

That is the glory of war.

❓ Q: Who inspired the poppy as a symbol of suffering in war?
A: John Alexander McCrae.

Lieutenant Colonel McCrae wrote this poem in 1915 after the death and burial of his friend Lieutenant Alex Helmer. It was written upon a scrap of paper in the back of a medical field ambulance and was published in *Punch* magazine. Lieutenant Colonel McCrae died in Boulogne in 1918 of pneumonia.

> *In Flanders fields the poppies blow*
> *Between the crosses, row on row,*
> *That mark our place; and in the sky*
> *The larks, still bravely singing, fly*
> *Scarce heard amid the guns below.*
> *We are the Dead. Short days ago*
> *We lived, felt dawn, saw sunset glow,*
> *Loved, and were loved, and now we lie,*
> *In Flanders fields.*
> *Take up quarrel with the foe:*
> *To you from falling hands we throw*
> *The torch; be yours to hold it high.*
> *If ye break faith with us who die*
> *We shall not sleep, though poppies grow*
> *in Flanders fields.*

❓ Q: Who started Poppy Day?
A: A group of French war widows.

In 1921 these women travelled to England and took poppies with them. They suggested the poppies could be sold to raise funds for those who had been injured by the war. It is indeed a noble ideal, and it was not thought up by generals or politicians, but by that most civilised of all creatures — women.

Tax

Along with war, tax is the other great bane of humanity. They are more closely related than you would expect. In fact, they are blood brothers.

What is income tax?

A government protection racket.

A gang is defined as a group of persons associated for some (usually) criminal purpose. Gangsters are often involved in racketeering or extortion where they charge honest businesses a fee — protection money. The businesses are forced to pay, usually through a small percentage of their takings. If they don't pay up the gangsters threaten to *use force to make them pay.*

Most honest businesses act by persuasion: they offer goods for sale and the public willingly exchanges money for them. Businesses are formed by individuals or groups of individuals who wish to provide something valuable to others and get the reward. They are not gangs.

Governments *use force to make you pay* income tax. Therefore by the above definitions, are they gangs?

Q: Why was the Dobermann breed of dog established?
A: To collect tax.

The Dobermann dog is tall, sleek, muscular and intimidating. The breed was established by the German tax collector Ludwig Dobermann to frighten his clients into paying tax.

❓ Q: Were there taxes before income tax?
A: There have always been taxes going under one name or another.

Historically, those in power (kings, nobles and priests) placed a tithe (tax) of 10% on the production of those who actually did the work. Taxes were raised not because the king needed a new crown, but to fund going to war. In other words, so he could carry out a protection racket against other nations.

Every country and culture in the world has legal statutes prohibiting murder. However, governments will happily waive this as long as *foreigners* are killed in the act of war. This is okay.

Q: Why was income tax invented?

A: To fund war.

Q: Why was the United States formed?

A: In the spirit of rebellion against tax.

Income tax was invented by the British in 1799 to fight the Napoleonic Wars. Before this time, Britain had raised money from its colonies, especially the very productive ones in the US, by placing taxes on items such as sugar, glass, lead and (the final straw) tea, until the colonists eventually rebelled and in July 1776 issued the Declaration of Independence.

Q: Did the Americans raise taxes to fight the War of Independence?

A: Actually, the founding fathers were honourable men and stuck to their principles.

The new country refused to resort to the devil of taxation to fund the war. It survived on loans from merchants, and on loans and gifts from other nations, and many of the soldiers fought without pay but with the promise of free land. They won, but unfortunately this story did not end happily ever after.

Q: Why not? They didn't, did they ... ?

A: In 1861 and 1862 Congress passed the first income tax laws.

Q: Why?

A: To fight another war.

This time it was the American Civil War.

Unfortunately, a very great tragedy had occurred at the birth of America. The founding fathers threw away the notes so that succeeding generations did not fully understand why they framed the Constitution the way they did, and unfortunately the tax wolf snuck back in the gate.

❓ Q: But how did income tax become the norm even when there were no wars?
A: By the infiltration of habit.

In Britain, income tax laws were passed, then repealed, then passed again. After a while people became so conditioned to paying income tax — even when there wasn't a war on — that by the 1880s income tax had become an institution.

In the US they held out a little longer. Congress did pass an income tax law, but the Supreme Court declared it to be unconstitutional. It was not until February 1913 that the 16th Amendment of the Constitution finally made everyone liable for income tax.

Amendment is a euphemism for alteration. Congress were violating their own constitution. The land of the free was a little less free.

❓ Q: Where does the philosophy behind income tax come from?
A: Oddly enough, the modern use of it comes from communism.

The original philosophy of kings was to collect taxes from the poor. The modern philosophy, as propounded by Karl Marx in his communist manifesto *Das Kapital*, is to tax the rich instead. *Take from those that have and give to those who need.* That's our modern welfare state. That's communism.

The problem with the theory is that the rich get to be rich by being smart, and they can employ smart accountants who minimise their tax bill.

As the common people started making more money, the government looked to tax them more. In 1943 the US Government was desperate for money because (yes, you've guessed it) there was another war on.

Then somebody had the bright idea to take the tax money straight out of a worker's pay packet, instead of assessing a worker's income only once a year, and Pay As You Earn (PAYE) was born.

❓ Q: Could you just summarise this?
■ A: Only too happy to.

Originally, everybody owned what they produced.

Then chiefs were invented and started taking a share.

After that, kings were invented who sent out tax collectors to take their share, usually 10%, but this went up in times of war.

Once people discovered they were being ripped off, democracy was invented and now people were able to choose who was ripping them off.

The tax collectors stopped knocking on their doors with fierce-looking dogs and instead the money was taken straight out of workers' pay packets, *before they even had the chance to look at it or touch it.*

In Western countries these days, income tax is on average around 20%. In other words, a worker works one day a week for the government. Added to this are various other taxes and duties that people are paying for, which bring the real figure paid to the government closer to between 30 and 40%.

So we can all look back with nostalgia to the days when the evil kings were taking only 10%.

? Q: What should be done about income tax?
A: It should be abolished.

It is the burden of everyone. If there has to be a contribution to the state, then taxing expenditure through the sale of goods or services is the only one that is fair to all.

Chapter 5
The Big Questions

How big is the universe?

A Infinite.

There are billions of galaxies in the universe. Our galaxy (from the Greek *galaktos* for 'milk') is like a giant spiral approximately 100,000 light years wide. Our Sun is one of about one billion stars in our galaxy. Then there are all the other galaxies ...

So, the universe is pretty big. I don't know anyone who has been to the end of the universe and back again.

Q: What is the universe made of?
A: Matter, energy, space and time.

Originally, the Greek philosopher Empedocles stated that there were four elements: earth, air, fire and water. The four basic constituents are:

◇ matter, which is solid (objects);

◇ energy, which flows and changes (creating motion);

◇ space, which is all the gaps between the objects and the energy;

◇ time, which is now. Whoops, that now is now then. I mean this now now. It moved again. Well, you know what I mean ...

Q: What is the Earth?
A: A big rock that floats in space.

The Earth takes a year to amble around the Sun. It is held in orbit by the gravitational pull of our Sun and by other planetary bodies. The universe is a giant network of flows, all holding each other in suspense and moving at the same time.

Q: What does the Earth consist of?
A: Rock and water floating on fire.

The oceans cover nearly three-quarters of the surface of the Earth. That leaves about a quarter of it for land and since just under a quarter of that is uninhabitable desert, that doesn't leave much room for land-dwellers!

The Earth's crust is of varying thickness, but is usually at least 18 miles (30 km).In the middle is a molten core (magma) which lets off steam every so often by shooting up through volcanoes (named after Vulcan, the Roman god of fire).

According to the theory of continental drift proposed by the geologist Alfred Wegener in 1915, the crust consists of about 15 huge geological plates which move upon the magma a bit like rafts on a lake.

The evidence of slow fender-benders is all around us in the form of mountain ranges, such as the Himalayas or the Southern Alps of New Zealand. But don't worry, the US is not going to crash into Europe any day soon as the plates move very slowly; maybe a centimetre or two a year.

Rock is essentially cooled magma. On top of it is a skin-deep coating of soil on which plants grow and little children build sandcastles.

❓ Q: What is life?
▪ A: That which animates the physical world.

Matter, energy, space and time are all lifeless. The difference between these lifeless things and life is that living things have choice. A tree has life and so its branches can twist towards the Sun.

❓ Q: What's the difference between plants and animals?
▪ A: Animals are footloose and fancy-free.

Plants are generally rooted to the ground. Animals can move around.

❓ Q: What's the difference between animals and humans?
▪ A: Humans have intellect.

Dolphins are intelligent, but they can't play chess.

Gorillas have been taught vocabularies of several hundred words in sign language. They have been known to place two words in relation to each other to make up a concept they have not been taught. They can even understand certain abstract concepts, such as 'sad'. But they can't build bridges, design complex machines or engage in long intellectual discussion about refined subjects like love and football.

Okay, football is not that refined. An ape could probably understand it.

But could an ape understand art?

? Q: What is art?
A: Quality of communication.

You can live in a cold and draughty cave. Or you can use the art of architecture to build a palace.

You could not tell someone how you feel about them. Or you can sing them a song of your love.

At one concert in Germany, Luciano Pavarotti received 165 curtain calls and was applauded for an hour and seven minutes.

? Q: What is the purpose of art?
A: To uplift the individual and shape the culture.

Culture is created by its artists. They evolve the culture by introducing new ideas. They uplift the spirit.

? Q. What is Hollywood?
A. Hollywood is a marketing machine that supplies hope.

Hollywood is a dream factory. At its inception most business moguls thought it was beneath them to engage in this shoddy new industry where people sat in a dark theatre and watched a flickering image, but through great comedians like Charlie Chaplin and Buster Keaton, film became the art form of the common people. Hollywood invented stars and it encourages people to reinvent themselves.

? Q: What is a mind?
A: Your own personal film.

The mind consists of mental image pictures of everything you have recorded through your perceptions. You can run it backwards or forwards like a film.

? Q: But who is the projectionist? And who is the director?
A: You are.

You are the star of your own life.

❓ Q: Is there more to life than meets the eye?
■ A: I certainly hope so.

There are some things that are very hard to explain, if you stick to the more-serious-than-thou reality which is often drummed into us at school.

For example, in 1898 Morgan Robertson wrote a novel called *The Wreck of the Titan*, about a huge ship that struck an iceberg. Fourteen years later on 15 April 1912, the *Titanic* hit an iceberg. In 1935 a ship called the *Titanian* almost hit an iceberg but was saved by the premonition ofcrewman William Reeves who, shortly before the iceberg became visible, yelled out 'Danger ahead!'

Reeves was born on the day the *Titanic* sank.

❓ Q: Any other unusual occurrences?
■ A: Abraham Lincoln foretold his own death.

It had been arranged that on the evening of 14 April 1865, which was Good Friday, Lincoln and his wife Mary would go to the theatre with the daughter of a senator and her fiancé.

Mrs Lincoln tried to beg off. Lincoln said that he was tired, but wanted to go because he needed a good laugh.

A few days before, Mary noticed that her husband looked dreadfully solemn. Lincoln admitted that he had had a bad dream the previous night. This is what he told her:

> *I had been up waiting for important dispatches from the front. I could not have been long in bed when I fell into a slumber, for I was weary. I soon began to dream. There seemed to be a death-like stillness about me. Then I heard subdued sobs, as if a number of people were weeping. I thought I had left my bed and wandered downstairs. There the silence was broken by the same pitiful sobbing, but the mourners were invisible. I went from room to room; no living person was in sight, but the same mournful sounds of distress met me as I passed along ... Determined to find*

the cause of the state of things so mysterious and so shocking, I kept on until I arrived at the East Room which I entered. There I met with sickening surprise. Before me was a catafalque, on which rested a corpse wrapped in funeral vestments. Around it were stationed soldiers who were acting as guards.

'Who is dead in the White House?' I demanded of one of the soldiers.

'The President,' was his answer; 'he was killed by an assassin.'

On 14 April, while Lincoln was absorbed in the play, the footman allowed a well-known actor called John Wilkes Booth to enter the presidential box. Booth immediately placed a single-shot Derringer pistol behind Lincoln's left ear and fired.

The President died at 7.22 the next morning.

Q: Is there life on other planets?
A: Apart from the alien who lives in my garden shed ...

... there is the well documented story of the Dogon tribe in Africa long ago. When Western explorers first arrived in the area, the Dogon told them that they had been visited by aliens who told them they came from a planet which took 50 years to orbit around their sun, Sirius. The Dogon repeated this story to the first Western explorers, who probably did not believe them.

But later, powerful telescopes were invented that could gaze further into the depths of the galaxy and they revealed that there was a planet that took 50 years to orbit Sirius.

Q: Do UFOs exist?
A: That's a tricky question.

Because, of course, as soon as you identify an unidentified flying object, then it ceases to be an unidentified flying object, doesn't it? And if you fail to identify it, then you can't really claim to know what you are unidentifying either.

Seriously, there have been many accounts of UFOs and one of the most authoritative was by Gordon Cooper, one of the seven astronauts chosen to train for the very first space programme.

Their story was featured in the film *The Right Stuff* (Cooper was played by Dennis Quaid). Before they became astronauts, they were all fighter pilots and in his autobiography, Cooper tells of flying patrols over Europe and how he and other highly trained pilots would talk among themselves about unidentified craft in the sky. These objects possessed both a speed and manoeuvrability that made their own state-of-the-art fighter planes seem like old biplanes.

Q: Is there life on other planets?
A: What you are really asking is, 'Are we the only ones to win the lottery of life?'

If you take the billions of planets in the universe and say that out all of them, there only happens to be one that has life on it, then mathematically those odds just don't add up.

I have toured around many small towns and it's amazing how many people I met who were convinced their own town was the best town in the world. Perhaps there are other planets around the galaxy whose inhabitants are convinced that theirs is the *only planet* with life on it too.

Q: What is religion?
A: A system of spiritual belief.

Ever since humans first evolved on this planet, several thousand years ago, we have believed in some form of spiritual existence beyond our current state of existence. We have used an enormous array of religions to try and explain this belief.

Q: Wait a minute, what about all the wars that have been fought over religion?
A: No war was ever started over religion.

Winston Churchill makes the same statement in the opening line of one of his books. People feel very strongly about their religions, and those people who bring about wars for their own gain use it as a means to stir things up. People can be as patriotic about their religion as they are about their country.

Q: Where did the modern 'religion' of materialism come from?
A: It was invented by rats.

There was this rat. There was also this frog. They were studied in 1879 by Professor Wilhelm Wundt at the University of Leipzig, because he reckoned that by investigating croaking and cheese eating, he would better understand people. From this, experimental psychology was born.

Psychology comes from the Greek *psyche* or 'spirit'. It was originally the study of the spirit, although it now generally denies the human spirit and contends that man is an animal.

The German chancellor of the time, Otto von Bismarck, used the power of his position to promote this principle, since an animal has no sense of values and therefore can be trained like a dog to fight in wars. Bismarck was the original architect of the German military machine, which would ultimately lead to the two world wars of the twentieth century.

The materialist believes that only matter matters.

Q: Is there a human spirit?
A: If there isn't, it's all a bit of a waste of time really, isn't it?

Q: Is there life after death?
A: There are strong indications of it.

I wrote a book once about a girl, Kirsty Bentley, who was murdered, supposedly while walking her dog in Ashburton, New Zealand. When her mother Jill and I took that same walk, strange things happened. A freak blizzard blew up and fantails flitted around a tree nearby.

One traditional Maori belief is that this bird is a symbol of reincarnation.

Kirsty's body had been found under a tree elsewhere. When Jill visited the location some time after, a tree there had been full of fantails. But the birds were on one particular tree only: the one under which Kirsty's body had been found.

Soon after Kirsty died, a bird had entered the house of her best friend Lee-Anne and stayed there. The bird would perch on top of the sofa. There was also a cat in the house, which would sit on the lower part of the sofa. But it would not touch the bird.

The day after Kirsty's body was found, the cat killed the bird.

What kind of bird was it? You already know the answer.

It was a fantail.

? Q: Can a person go outside their body?
A: Apparently so.

The original meaning of the word 'ecstasy' is 'standing outside oneself'. Many people, when they have experienced intense happiness, have reported feeling as though they are outside their body.

? Q: Should we be frightened of ghosts?
A: Not really.

Maybe ghosts are simply disembodied spirits who take the definition of being homeless a little bit further.

? Q: What happens after you die?
A: What you believe depends on your religion.

Some say you go to heaven. Or hell. For materialists, their credit cards get cancelled.

If you were to boil down the body it would reduce to a cup of lard and a bucket of water.

Olaf 'the Stout' Haraldsson II was a Viking king of the tenth century who became a Christian. Inexplicably, his hair and nails continued to grow for months after he was killed in battle. When people visited his tomb, they found that they were cured of their ailments. Olaf was later made patron saint of Norway.

The most embarrassing death ever was maybe the one suffered by Edmund Ironside, who was sitting over a toilet pit at the time. Unknown to him, his assassin was right there with him, up to his neck in (you know what) and from that stinky place, the assassin thrust his sword and that was that.

When people choose to get cremated, their ashes will weigh around 9 pounds (4 kg). So if that's the body taken care of, where does the personality go? Where does all the creativity and experience go? Where does all the laughter go?

❓ Q: Have we had past lives?
A: Theoretically, if a spirit could survive death, it would have to precede birth too.

There are many stories that support past lives. It would also explain how Mozart, without any education or training in his life, could compose entire symphonies at the age of five.

In the US during the early twentieth century there was a Christian preacher from the Midwest. One day a young girl in his congregation told him she was worried about her children. As she was far too young to be a mother, he humoured her by listening, but noted that her concern seemed genuine and that she was able to give him specific details, including the names of the children and exactly where they were located. This was in a town not too far from the preacher's, so he decided to visit.

When he got there he found the family exactly where the young girl had said they would be, and the names of the children were just as the little girl had said. Their mother had died about the same time as the young girl had been born.

The preacher then travelled back to his hometown and went to see the young girl, telling her that the father had remarried and that everybody in the family was doing well.

The girl thanked him and never mentioned the subject again.

❓ Q: Who am I?
A: Whoever you are, you are unique.

❓ Q: Who is God?
A: This is the final question.

This is the final question in this book, and perhaps the final question of life itself.

Turn the page to discover the answer.

Only you can answer
that question.